VICTORIA POLICE

Office of the Chief Commissioner

Police Headquarters

Melbourne, Vic. 3000

23 November, 1990

Senior Constable L.N. McCULLOCH, 24205,
CIB (CARLTON).

Dear Senior Constable McCulloch,

It gives me great pleasure to inform you that you have been awarded the Highly Commended Certificate for "dedication to duty, courage and restraint in the rescue of a child and the apprehension of a violent and dangerous offender at Carlton on 25th September, 1990."

I trust that news of the award of the Certificate gives you and your family as much pleasure as it gives me to convey the news to you.

You will be advised in due course, of the arrangements for presentation of the Certificate.

Congratulations on an excellent effort.

Yours sincerely,

K. GLARE, APM. O.St.J.
CHIEF COMMISSIONER

NO MERCY

NO MERCY

CONFESSIONS OF AN UNDERCOVER COP

BY LACHLAN McCULLOCH

JOHN BLAKE

Published by John Blake Publishing Ltd,
3, Bramber Court, 2 Bramber Road,
London W14 9PB, England

www.blake.co.uk

First published in paperback in 2003

ISBN 1 84454 011 1

British Library Cataloguing-in-Publication Data:

A catalogue record for this book is available from the British Library.

Design by www.envydesign.co.uk

Printed in Great Britain by BookMarque

1 3 5 7 9 10 8 6 4 2

Papers used by John Blake Publishing are natural, recyclable products made from
wood grown in sustainable forests. The manufacturing processes conform to the
environmental regulations of the country of origin.

Every attempt has been made to contact the relevant copyright-holders, but some
were unobtainable. We would be grateful if the appropriate people could contact us.

DEDICATION

*To my father, Rob, who taught
me right from wrong and to my wife,
Bernadette, who made sure I
remembered the difference.*

FOREWORD

I was a member of the police force for almost sixteen years, working undercover and in the drug squad.

I loved (almost) every minute of it, but the most exciting time for me was working around Fitzroy Street, St Kilda – known as 'The Street'. It was never-ending, full-on policing – every day was filled with drama, tragedy and black humour.

This is a composite picture of my experiences and those of my colleagues. Angus is a policeman who could have worked in any major city. His partner, Darren, is a mixture of every policeman and woman I ever worked with.

These are the stories police tell each other when they think no-one else is listening.

All the names and addresses used in this book are fictitious, so don't bother sueing or I will deny it all.

CONTENTS

chapter 1

THE ROAD TO THE STREET

'Never expect people to react the way you think they will'

COPPERS see a lot of unhappy endings. Ambos, doctors and nurses see bad shit, too, but mostly it's the cops who get there first. Some have their own way of dealing with the really bad stuff. Some never do.

I'll never forget the afternoon I was driving down Fitzroy Street, St Kilda, with my partner Sandy, when a radio call came over saying 'Shots fired in the vicinity of the St Kilda Cafe.' We were close by. I screamed the car to a halt and double-parked in front of the cafe. I walked towards the front door, gun drawn.

As I got near the door I saw a small-time junkie crim called Terry crawling along on his elbows inside the cafe toward the doorway. Behind him were two trails of blood, like tram tracks. The blood led back to where two slip-on shoes were in front of the counter. They marked the spot where Terry had been kneecapped a few seconds before. Trouble was, it had been done with a shotgun at close range, and it had almost blown his legs off.

Kneecapping is normally done with a pistol as a gangster's payback. It's not meant to kill people. Only a maniac would use a shotgun. Terry was blown out of his shoes, poor bastard.

Sandy grabbed the radio and called for an ambulance. The area was safe, as the offender had gone. I stopped Terry as he crawled through the tassels at the doorway and knelt down. He crawled onto my lap. He was becoming weaker by the second. He looked up into my face and whispered, 'Tank said I owed him eighty bucks, but that's shit. I paid him. I'm not a dog, but Tank's killed me.'

I squeezed his shoulder and said, 'You'll be right, I've got you, it's okay.'

He squeezed me back weakly and then he just seemed to tune out. There was less and less, then there was nothing. I held his lifeless head and looked at our reflection in the window. He had bled to death. There was nothing I could do. I hated him and all crooks like him, but in this brief moment we were brothers in the same senseless world.

Ambulance men took him from me. I put out an urgent 'Keep a look out for' and an 'Approach with caution' warning to all members about Tank, a local lunatic who had supposedly fought in Vietnam although no-one knew, or cared, if it was true.

I automatically 'crime scened' the area and looked for witnesses. I noticed someone look at the front of my shirt. It had Terry's bloody hand prints all over it. I immediately ripped it off and threw it in a rubbish bin, exposing my shoulder holster with speed loader and cuffs attached.

As I walked away from the bin I stopped and looked back at it. Suddenly, I realised what a cold-hearted, rotten thing I'd done. For a split-second I had actually been pissed off at the poor dead bastard for bleeding on me.

I wanted to reach back in the bin and get the shirt, as if that would somehow make it better. Then I thought: I'm a cop. I'm supposed to be a hard son-of-a-bitch. I walked a couple of shops away to a clothes store and bought another shirt. Why? Because I thought that's what a tough copper should do.

That night on the way home I stopped and ate a pizza with the lot and double anchovies. And I told myself, not for the first time, that if you can eat a pizza afterwards, everything must be all right. That it's just another day working The Street.

To this day whenever I see slip-on shoes I think of how peculiar Terry's pair looked that day on the floor in the cafe.

Anyway …

AS a young boy I cried during every episode of *Lassie* and *Kimba the White Lion.*

I get emotional about most things. I never had the makings of a hard-boiled copper, but being a round peg that didn't fit in the police department's square hole would prove to be a great advantage.

I went to a boys' private grammar school and left at the end of year eleven to do a variety of jobs, mostly selling one thing or another.

I sold cars, fishing tackle and even pine tree plantations. It turned out to be great training for a job I didn't know I even wanted.

I later sold myself, undercover. I found it easier than pine tree plantations. When you're undercover, first you have to sell yourself to the crooks and then sell them a story they'll believe.

If you're believed and accepted, you're in. The thing is, it's not acting. The minute you act, you're not real. When a crook asks you a question, looking for a real person, he must reach out and touch you, if there is nothing there, you're 'blown', but if he finds a real person, you're in. Cops are like school teachers. Nobody thinks they're real people. If you go undercover and give a bad act most crooks will see right through it. We can all pick a fake, but give them a real person and they are stuffed.

EACH year in my late teens my father bought me a plane ticket to anywhere I wanted to go. I mostly chose exotic fishing locations in Northern Australia.

I went fishing for two weeks at a fishing lodge in the Gulf of Carpentaria on my eighteenth birthday. For my nineteenth birthday I got a return ticket to London – originally for three months. At my going away party, I overheard my father tell my uncle that I wouldn't last ten minutes over there because I couldn't look after myself.

I stayed in Europe for twelve months. I travelled around; I coached tennis for a few months in England at the Harpendon Lawn Tennis Club, worked in hotels, drove around Europe for more than seven months and worked the rest to pay for it.

I bought a vehicle with another Aussie and a Kiwi – it cost us five hundred pounds – and after driving it for a year I paid a bloke twelve quid to tow it away.

I was never exposed to criminals in all my upbringing and had never met a police officer on duty until I was pulled up for speeding when I was about nineteen.

My opinion of policemen, back then, was they were basically arrogant arseholes … and now I'm sitting here after sixteen years in the job knowing that first impressions aren't always wrong.

With some great exceptions, I still think some of them can still be arrogant and, at times, arseholes. But now I think I know why they end up like that.

MY parents had a close friend they had known for many years. His name was Phil Watson and they'd met him in Queensland fifty years ago. He was a big Queensland policeman who would visit Victoria every few years and when he did, he came to our home. He didn't inspire me to join the job and I don't even remember him telling me old cop stories.

He died about twelve years ago. My parents told me he always thought that he was the reason I joined the job and I saw no reason to spoil his illusion.

He was a very large, very nice man, but I was never very close to him. I remember he came to my graduation at the Victoria Police Academy. That was the last time I ever remember speaking to him.

He said something like, 'Angus, just remember, always do the right thing.' I remember thinking that it was a ridiculous thing to say to a policeman. Now, I know exactly why he said it. It is always so easy in 'The Job' to do the wrong thing. But let's not get ahead of the story …

The fact is, I never dreamt of being a policeman until I was about twenty-one when I met a guy at a party – a fancy dress turn in North Carlton. He was dressed as Clint Eastwood in some spaghetti western, wearing a heavy-knitted wool poncho, a cowboy hat and a beard.

He was the first cop I had ever really spoken to in a social way. He was a homicide cop and I asked him what it was like. He said it was just fantastic. He drove fast cars, caught crooks and just generally had a ball.

I was hooked.

I made the decision and did a course on how to pass the entrance exam and ended up getting in. I walked into the Victoria Police Academy on the fourth of January, 1984. I did my five months there and I came just about last in my squad, thirty-ninth out of forty-one. Not a brilliant start – and a sign that as a copper, I was a bit different from most of the others.

At my thirtieth birthday I had about sixty guests, and only one was a copper. His name was Darren. We forged our friendship during the St Kilda days.

BEING an undercover operative throughout most of my career meant that I spent the whole time trying not to be a cop.

This meant that my whole demeanour was not one of a typical cop. The consequence was that for a lot of cops, I didn't really fit in. Many typical arrogant cops had no idea where I was coming from. I didn't play football and go to the pub after work with them. In many ways, I was a bit of an outsider.

What really fucked them was that I caught heaps of crooks. That's because I understood crooks. Real crooks could see through the 'Would be if they could be – I'm a legend' type of cop. Crooks knew they could buy them a few drinks – or, better still, get them a 'drink card' at a night club – and those cops would be in their pocket without them even knowing.

What crooks didn't like was cops who paid for their own drinks, or even bought them some. Cops that couldn't be given a head job by a prostitute while waiting for a bust to go down, couldn't be given a diamond ring for their girlfriend, or a stereo, a TV set or a new watch. Crooks hated not knowing where they stood – or, worse, knowing they stood as nothing but a crook, pure and simple. Maintaining the boundaries made the cop dangerous and totally unpredictable to them.

The typical arrogant 'cockheaded' detective got his information from crooks by befriending them, or trying to. For a lot of them it's cool to have crooks as friends and associates, and most crooks like the idea of knowing detectives, too. These cops can be heard to say, 'You don't find crooks sitting in church.' Whereas I say, crooks are crooks and cops are cops. There should be a difference. Too often there wasn't.

When a cop meets a crook, the crook must instantly know the difference. The difference between right and wrong and good and evil.

If the cop befriends the crook, the difference is lost, or at least blurred. Wrong becomes acceptable. The cop then finds that wrong can become valuable. Mostly the crook pays with information.

I preferred to get my information by fear. Not fear of personal violence, but fear of the professional detective, fear of me 'working' on them.

I found that crooks respected cops who would catch them lawfully, thus liking or respecting them for just doing the job. Deep down, most crooks would like to be detectives, or undercover cops. Crooks feared me 'setting them up' – not with fake evidence, but by organising a prostitute or another criminal to do a drug deal at a certain location, at a certain time with a certain crook, thus obtaining real evidence by arresting them in the middle of the deal. I would organise a straight-up pinch and that assured respect and assured fear – thus assuring good current information regarding current criminal activity.

Some cops would obtain information from crooks by threatening to set them up. Some cops might just pick up the crook in The Street, (after warnings to give them information or else) put them in the car and start singing 'Happy Birthday to you', then giving the crook a 'birthday present,' such as a quantity of drugs, drug-associated equipment such as scales or bags, then charging them with trafficking. This was commonly called 'loading up'.

IN my early days in the job I was directing traffic at the intersection of Swanston Street and Flinders Street outside the clocks. It's the biggest intersection in Melbourne. We had to turn the lights off during each peak hour period and control it by hand.

I was being abused by motorists all the time and it didn't take me long to get jack of it. The first time you do traffic duty it is terrifying – you are frightened, then you put your hand up to order people to stop and they do just that. You quickly learn you are The Man.

I remember waiting for certain motorists to indicate to me where they wanted to go, if they wanted to go straight ahead I would stop them and make them turn left or right. If they wanted to turn, I would make them go straight ahead.

I only did it because I could.

You would see some bloke in a suit looking at you like you were a pain in the neck and slowing them from getting where they wanted to go. They were the type I would make go the wrong way. I recall looking at my open hand (the palm with all fingers together) and thinking 'Christ, that's powerful.'

To a young policeman, the uniform is very powerful. I don't know why I have included this little story because it doesn't really make me look good. But it's the truth, and most cops know it in their hearts. I included it because it's part of a learning curve. When you get a fast car, you want to see how fast you can drive it; when you get a new golf driver, you want to see how far you can hit with it. When you leave the Police Academy you are given a uniform and power and you want to push against the limits to see how far you can go. In the end most police grow out of it.

But some don't.

VERY early on, about a week out of the Police Academy, I was working with an old senior constable when we got a radio message, 'We have been notified by the morgue that they have just identified a body, being one Stanley John Davis. He suicided off the Westgate Bridge last night. Please attend 15 Smith Street, Richmond, and notify next of kin, Ruth Davis.'

The senior constable said, 'Will this be your first death message?'

I went into vapour lock. My mouth went all dry and I could hardly breathe, I was so shocked at the thought of delivering a death message. We practised at the academy, but this was for real. I knew I would have to do it one day, but not in my worst nightmare did I think it would happen after only just one week on the road. My experienced partner gave me all the advice. Most of it was things like, 'Slowly lead up to it. First introduce yourself, then say you have bad news and slowly lead up to the fact that he has died. Take a deep breath – you'll be right.' I secretly hoped he would take pity on me and do it himself, but I knew it was going to be up to me.

We both walked up to the door. I knocked. A well-presented, middle aged women answered.

I said, 'Hello, I'm Constable Angus and …'

She interrupted, saying 'What's the matter?'

She was full-on, right on top of me, and cut me off in the middle of my hastily-prepared speech.

I tried to gather my thoughts. 'Well,' she snapped, stopping me in my tracks again. 'Well, what is it?'

I said, 'Well, we um, got a message from the morgue.'

She said, 'The morgue?'

I thought, 'Shit, morgue is a bad word.'

She screamed, 'Morgue! You get a message from the morgue and you come here to my front door. Why?'

I said, 'Well, your husband is at the morgue.'

She said, 'My husband is at the morgue sending you a message to come here. What message?'

I was out of my depth and sinking faster than a Russian sub.

I looked at my partner and so did she. 'What is this bloke on about?' she asked.

The experienced senior connie was a picture or calmness and compassion. 'I'm sorry to inform you that your husband has passed away,' he said gently. 'He died last night.'

She didn't even draw breath. 'He didn't wreck the car, did he?' she said. 'It's a Subaru Liberty station wagon. Where is it?' It had never gone like that out at the academy. I stood there with my mouth open. I was in greater shock than she was, and definitely more emotional. It turned out that her husband had left her several months earlier and she had been trying to get the car from him ever since. I learnt a valuable lesson that day. Never use the word 'morgue' in a prepared speech leading up to a death message – and never expect people to react the way you think they will.

I WAS keen from the word go to become a detective. That's all I wanted to do – to be a detective and catch real crooks.

I became the first one in my squad to become a detective, three years and four months into The Job.

After leaving the academy I wanted to go to the busiest station I could. In those days trainees weren't allowed to go to St Kilda, so I transferred to the nearest place to St Kilda that would take me, which was Richmond. At that time the talk of the town was Dennis Allen, Peter Allen, Kath Pettingill, in fact the whole Pettingill family. They were probably the worst criminal family in Australia and later implicated in the murders of two young cops, Senior Constable Steven Tynan and Constable Damian Eyre, in Walsh Street.

Dennis was reporting twice a day for trafficking heroin and heaps of serious assault charges.

Kath was reporting daily for possessing a machine gun and heroin trafficking. Every shift you just drove around looking for taxis and movement in the Stephenson Street and Chestnut Street area where the Pettingills and Allens were selling drugs. We just had to pull over anybody driving in those streets that looked suspicious. Nearly every time they either had $90 to buy heroin or they had heroin in their possession that they had just bought.

They'd also take heaps of stolen goods and jewellery to

various places. They'd be in stolen cars at times. The fact is, the area around the Pettingills was just full of shit. Every shift you just caught crook after crook and the only thing that held you back was the time it took to process them. You could either lock them up and remand them or, if they gave you information, they got bail. It was like going to your favourite fishing spot: you rarely came home disappointed.

I RECALL as a trainee opening the front door to the Richmond Police Station for Kath Pettingill. I didn't know it was the woman who gave birth to most of the biggest crime family in Melbourne; I'd only been in the job a couple of days and as she walked up to the door, I just thought, 'Here's a lovely old lady'.

She was about fifty at the time, but she looked older. As I saw her coming, I'd just walked out of the station, so I stopped and held the door open for her.

She looked at me and said, 'What the fuck do you think you're doing?' Then she knocked on the window which is right next to the door (the station's still the same now) and a policeman in the watchhouse area opened it.

Kath then called to the police inside, 'have a look at this fuck'n bloke.' And I'll never forget, there were about three or four coppers peeping out of the window looking at me holding the door open, and I was just in shock.

I couldn't believe this old lady was swearing her head off and I couldn't understand why it was so interesting for everyone to come and look at me holding the door open.

She finished up by saying, 'Anyway, thanks love' and walked in to sign the bail book for heroin trafficking and possessing a machine gun.

I turned to my partner and said, 'What the fuck was that all about?' He just laughed and laughed and said to me, 'That's Kath Pettingill, mate – hop in the car and I'll tell you all about her.'

That was my very first meeting with Kath.

It's funny, you know. Nine years later I worked undercover and Kath introduced me to her son Trevor Pettingill and his associates. I sent sixteen of them to jail for a total of forty-two years, including Kath herself for nine months.

In the end I opened another door for her ... a prison door. Thanks, love.

AFTER about two weeks at Richmond I was driving past a park and there was an old undercoat grey panel van pulled over on the side of the road with two people in it, so we pulled up behind them.

My partner asked me to check them while he ran the registration through D24.

I looked in the driver's door window. There was a young bloke, about twenty odd, with his back to me.

He was leaning over to the passenger side and in the passenger seat was a young girl of about fifteen, leaning back in the seat looking at the roof. The guy in the driver's seat was leaning over her and injecting a blood and heroin filled syringe into her eye.

Obviously he'd already sucked up blood into the syringe and then mixed the heroin with the blood as they do, prior to injecting it. That's why I was confronted with this blood-filled syringe being slowly plunged into the base of her eye.

I couldn't believe it and just froze – it felt like ages. I couldn't grab him because he had the needle in her eye and I was scared that I would cause her more damage and I was torn between grabbing him and not grabbing him.

Anyway, it felt like ages but it was probably only a few seconds. He finished plunging this bloody liquid into the base of her eye.

I reached in and grabbed the hand holding the syringe, knocking the syringe onto the floor of the vehicle. I put my left arm around his throat, my elbow under his chin and dragged him backwards out the driver's window onto the road.

I knelt on the back of his head, pushing his face into the roadway, and handcuffed him. I dragged him over to the grass by his hair; I couldn't hear him screaming. By this time my partner jumped out to see what was going on.

As for the girl in the passenger seat, the heroin had basically gone straight into her brain and she was unconscious. We carried her limp body onto the verge next to the park. Next thing two girls in a passing car pulled up, jumped out and asked if they could help. I said, 'No, no. Please get in your car and leave.' They explained to me that they were nurses and could actually help, so I asked them to check the girl.

A few minutes later the ambulance arrived and injected her with Narcan, which instantly reverses the effects of the heroin. Meanwhile, I wanted to kill the bloke who had done the injecting. I dragged him over to the back of the divisional van, but my partner grabbed me by the arm and said, 'hang on a second', so I let him go. I put him on the ground again and walked back to the car to talk to my partner.

He said, 'Listen, have a look' and he held up his watch. It was 2.50pm and our shift ended at 3pm. It was a Sunday,

7am to 3pm shift. He said, 'Come on, we've got ten minutes 'til we knock off – it's Sunday, for fuck's sake'. I said, 'What, after what he did?' Even in those days the charge was 'Introduce a Drug into the Body of Another.'

He directed me to uncuff the guy and let him go. I did what I was told, walked back to the car and sat there in total disbelief.

Letting him go was against everything I believed in. I lost track of what I was all about. I was there to fight crime, not finish work on time.

Fighting real crime was far more important than anyone's private life. I was there to protect the community. This was not a job, it was The Job. I was not there for the pay and to clock on and clock off. If I wanted that I would have worked in a factory.

I had been selected to protect and preserve life and property. To me, then, one of the perks of The Job was receiving a wage.

I truly believed. Letting him go was condoning everything I was against. To a young cop like me it was devastating.

I left my girlfriend and I didn't feel anything for anyone for a while. Of course, there were no psychologists to see back then. That would be a sign of weakness.

At around this time I remember saying to my girlfriend 'I don't love you – I don't love anything or anyone.' I was left with just me. You saw so much shit and grief it just left you numb.

Eventually, I must have got my act together and carried on. I truly believed that I could actually make a difference. It sounds corny, but I did. Now, more than sixteen years later, I feel like an angry little ant. If I hadn't investigated and charged crooks, they wouldn't have wanted to kill me. Then the barristers wouldn't have abused me in open court and my superiors wouldn't have hassled me for paperwork.

Maybe I should have been a time server. Maybe I should have looked at my watch more often and realised it was ten to three and nearly knock-off time. Now it's quarter to midnight. It's always later than you think.

I WAS driving down a side street in the divisional van in broad daylight in the back streets of Richmond. I stopped the van in the middle of a small street because to my right was a pathetic drug-fucked, twenty-four-year-old female, stuck half way through a window, her legs and arse sticking out, wiggling, feebly struggling to extricate herself.

I parked, stepped out of the police car in the tiny side street and walked through the front gate up to the legs.

I said: 'It's okay, it's the police. You can come with us, we'll look after you.' I had to look at the badge on my shoulder to make sure I was a cop and not a social worker.

We removed her backwards out of the window. You could see the lock had been forced. I left my business card under the front door for the owner to ring me.

The druggie in our custody was a sorry sight. Dirty, smelly, I reckon she would have been a real looker in her day. She was twenty-four, but looked a rough forty. She was slim, with pert breasts, but had the heroin look – a haggard face, old before its time. I remember thinking that the face reflects the truth: You can hide it in the body, but the face shows the sorrow and the damage of drugs.

She had the sallow, gaunt, pitiful face of impending death. I recall thinking if I lock her up, I can help her live a little bit longer. She didn't appreciate that though. She was on a one-way trip and no well-meaning young copper was going to stop it.

My partner and I laughed as we helped her out of her predicament. But it wasn't funny at all, it was desperately sad.

To me, we were all in the same game, all working together. It starts with the crooks. Back then cops always gave them a few extra charges so the solicitor would look good when a few charges had to be dropped, thus allowing the crook to plead guilty without losing face. Every child wins a prize.

They were all stupid crooks with no credibility whatsoever – heroin-addicted, low-life, petty shitheads.

But sometimes we would have fun with them. The black humour was the only thing that kept you sane. I was known to say: 'You are not obliged to say anything, anything you say will be grossly exaggerated and used in evidence against you. Do you understand that?'

Or 'You're not obliged to say nothing, and anything you don't say will be grossly exaggerated and used in evidence against you. Do you understand that?'

They would say, 'That's not fair.'

I'd say, 'It's not meant to be, it's the law.'

I'd say, 'You're nothing but a criminamle.'

They'd say, 'I'm not a criminamle.'

I'd say, 'You can't even say it properly.'

When you're bored, processing crooks for petty offences, you say and do silly things. I always tried to make being arrested by me a funny and memorable experience. Some crooks catch on and know that being arrested is all part of being a crook. Others remained shitty, and dreamed of meeting you off-duty in a dark lane.

I HAD been in The Job for about two days when I was given the important task of picking up dinner from the Chinese takeaway in Chinatown. It was night shift and dinner was about 3am.

I picked it up and found myself in the city driving a real police car. I was all by myself when I stopped the marked police car in the middle of the road at the very top of Bourke Street.

I looked down the hill towards The Mall. I turned the blue lights and both sirens on, then planted the foot and roared down Bourke Street. It was fantastic, as the shop windows reflected the blue lights back towards me and the sound was amplified by the concrete arcades. It felt good. Now I was a cop.

Around this time, a month or so out of the academy, I was on night shift when I drove down to the local 7/11 store. As I drove the marked police sedan into the car park, I noticed three hotted-up old Holden hot rods.

A dozen or so young bucks were milling around. They all looked at me as I quietly parked the cop car next to them. I walked in to the store and did the toughest thing I could think of. I purchased a large multi-coloured, multi-flavoured 'Slurpie', walked outside and stepped back into the car.

I put it in reverse, and did a burnout, completing what is commonly called a 'reverse donut' so that a black cloud of smoke engulfed the bucks. I paused long enough to smile at them.

I only did it because I could. The 'Superman Suit' (the blue uniform) sometimes does that to kids out of the academy. I didn't think I represented the law in the early days. I tended to think I was the law.

I HAVE always enjoyed the odd Slurpie. I was buying heroin as an undercover (as Lenny Rogers) for about four months from several criminals. The worst of them was called 'Stacker' because they said he used to stack up dead bodies.

Anyway, I had bought about $50,000 worth of heroin and speed from him, and he finally had to be arrested by the Special Operations Group after I bought him a Slurpie at a 7/11 store in Preston. We were both arrested at the time as part of the cunning plan.

Stacker had to be held in custody for several hours before he was interviewed, as I had to complete five 'buy busts' that day. (Buy busts are when you buy drugs or similar, then arrest all involved).

When Stacker was finally interviewed, he just said 'no comment' when questioned at length. Finally, the investigator played his ace, when he said, 'I now must inform you that Lenny Rogers is, in fact, an undercover policeman'.

Stacker thought about that for a moment and said, 'Well, he's fucked then isn't he?' To him I was a drug trafficker first and foremost. He could not even contemplate the fact that I was a police officer acting undercover to collect evidence against him. I have found that undercover operatives tend to totally embarrass the hell out of crooks, who think they are so smart. Can you imagine how embarrassing being caught by an undercover operative actually is? It could get them drummed out of the union.

Most crooks think they can pick an undercover a mile away. When someone is caught, everyone thinks they are idiots, so some crooks get very pissed off. In my experience it is then that the undercover operative could be in danger, as the crook has lost 'face'. The only way to get 'face' back is to get back at the undercover. The undercover operative can then become a target. This is amplified if Asian targets are involved, as they seem to relish revenge. Maybe it's part of their criminal culture or maybe they are just bad losers.

It is as if some crooks think that undercover work is unfair. They get their wires crossed. They think that because the undercover has got close to them that they have been betrayed. They react as if the undercover is one of them who has turned into an informer and not a policeman who has gathered evidence against them. They sell smack and kill people and yet they think an undercover has broken the rules.

Give me a break.

chapter 2

FAIR WEATHER FRIENDS

'You'll have to harden up if you're gonna stay in this job, mate'

WHEN I finally got the chance to transfer to St Kilda I felt right at home. My life as a private schoolboy was a distant memory until I ran into a childhood friend. Greg had gone to my primary school and we hadn't seen each other for about fourteen years. His father owned the Silver Q pool parlour in the main shopping centre of Oakleigh. My father had recently retired as the managing director of a large car manufacturing company.

We often played games together in the playground and Greg accidentally broke one of my front teeth playing British Bulldog. I couldn't clean my teeth without thinking of him.

We used to race small sticks down a creek at the back of my house. He was tough; when I got picked on by the older kids in school I remember Greg protecting me, because we were mates. Even at that stage we were from different worlds.

Anyway, Greg was now a chronic junkie. One day while I was working the divisional van, he decided to rob the Commonwealth Bank in Fitzroy Street, St Kilda.

He was now a short, angry little man covered in tattoos, with a nose that looked like it had been regularly punched over the years. Greg enlisted his prostitute girlfriend Leanne, who had blonde hair with a bright red streak through it; she came along to be 'lookout'.

Greg didn't have a gun or a knife, but he did have a paint spatula, which sort of looked like a knife if you were short sighted. I don't know if he wanted to rob the bank or paint it.

He made sure there were no cops about and walked into the bank. The branch was packed with customers, as it was lunch time. Greg had never worked a day in his life so he didn't realise that this was the bank's busiest time.

He needed money that minute so he didn't let the crowds worry him. He saw there were large queues in front of each teller, so he paused at the rear of one of them, then strode forward to commit his armed robbery. He shoved an old lady out of the way and pushed his paint spatula forward under his jacket, but he was so short the young teller couldn't see the bulge.

He said, 'Listen, I want …'

At that moment a large male (straight off a building site) standing in the queue decided that a little shitty-looking short arse wasn't going to push in and get served before him, so he leant forward, grabbed Greg by the back of the neck and said, 'I don't care what you want, you worm, wait your turn.'

This bloke then physically placed Greg at the back of the queue. The would-be-bandit was extremely embarrassed, he bent forward and looked out the glass door of the bank to make sure his 'lookout', not to mention girlfriend, hadn't seen what happened.

Reassured by the fact that she was still madly looking up and down the street, he changed his plans. He took a deep breath then tapped the shoulder of the guy standing in front of him and, while pushing the spatula forward under his jacket, quietly said, 'Give me all your money.'

The guy said, 'That's what I'm waiting for.' Greg hadn't worked out that if you wanted to rob a bank customer it would be better to wait until they had withdrawn their money.

The guy then produced $3.70 from his pocket and Greg grabbed it and ran out of the bank.

The bandit and his accomplice then ran off together, thus disclosing to all that Leanne was his lookout. The plan was for Leanne to just walk off, but the sight of Greg running was too much. She ran with him. You may have worked out by now that this couple were no Bonnie and Clyde.

I heard the 'Armed Robbery In Progress' call come over the radio. Their description followed. We knew immediately it was Leanne. Even in the freak show that was St Kilda there weren't too many blonde 'crows' with a red streak through their hair.

It was well-known to all St Kilda police that she would put out for the latest 'hot' crook in St Kilda for nothing.

We all knew she had been pounding Greg for about a week. People like Greg only lasted about a week because she earned $1000 a night. This often upset young crooks; being a pimp wasn't macho enough, and so they'd pull stupid armed robberies.

My partner and I arrested them within ten minutes, but I didn't want to interview him because we had grown up together. Greg kept on pleading with me to let him go; I just ignored him.

About a month later he was on remand, being held at the Prahran police station lock-up when I had about the tenth police officer come up to me and tell me that Greg was bragging to all the crooks and every copper he met that he grew up with me and we were the best of friends.

As I was a police officer and he was a heroin-addicted armed robber, albeit with a paint spatula, I thought it was time to have a chat.

One Sunday when it was very quiet and no other crooks could see me talking to him (for his sake) I arranged with the sergeant in charge at the time for me to go into his cell for a private chat.

I walked into his cell and he was really happy to see me. We shook hands.

His handshake was strong and firm; it was the sort of handshake that meant true mateship. My handshake was soft and sad, it made me feel guilty. I don't know why, because I hadn't done anything wrong. I was the law and he was well out of order.

I talked to him about how we grew up together and had been really good friends. Greg started recalling some old stories. Together we laughed and I fed him smokes.

I chewed a piece of toilet paper and threw it; it stuck on the lens of the video camera installed on the roof. The sergeant must have seen me throw it because no-one came into the cell.

I removed a small hip flask of Southern Comfort from my inside jacket pocket and handed it to Greg. Then came the hard part, as I tried to explain that we had taken different paths and that we were always from different worlds. I told him how I would always remember our friendship and I also explained that our friendship was over from that moment.

We shook hands overhand style. I shook it firmly and I squeezed his shoulder with my left hand. I truly meant it this time. I felt my lower lip quiver.

I started to walk out of the cell, opened the door and turned back to Greg. In a low, serious tone I said, 'Now don't ever mention my name again.'

He looked at me. That look made me feel like his last friend had just deserted him, but the truth was that he deserted himself when he got on the gear. Greg was already low on friends and he didn't need this. As I walked away from the cell I felt like I had just taken my dog to the vet and had it put down.

I have never seen or heard of Greg again. Leanne died of a heroin overdose about six months later.

A PARTICULAR cafe in St Kilda is the most well-known cafe in Victoria, if not Australia – not for cappuccinos but for for selling heroin. The cafe owners charged heroin traffickers $20 (pre-GST) an hour to sell heroin from their tables.

The owner of the cafe was losing so many spoons to heroin addicts – who used them to mix and inject heroin – that he drilled a small hole in the middle of each one. Not one of those spoons has ever been stolen since.

The cafe closed its doors for business for one minute as a sign of respect in remembrance of Leanne. This meant a lot to all the street kids and heroin-addicted prostitutes. It meant that you had been a somebody in a world of nobodies.

At Leanne's inquest it was discovered the caretaker in her hostel accommodation had made a statement disclosing the fact that he had sexual intercourse with her around 8am the morning she died.

Unfortunately, the State Coroner made a statement disclosing the fact that she had died of a heroin overdose about 10pm the night before.

Her dubious chastity was not safe, even in death. Her twin sister Simone, also a prostitute, had a very bad attitude towards police. She was foul mouthed, and could never come to terms with the fact that coppers charge people who commit crime because that's their job.

In the years afterwards, some officers were heard to say to Simone that her sister was a 'dead root.' This was not in the best taste, I thought.

In the St Kilda days, I can't recall meeting any criminals who weren't junkies. Armed robberies would go off at the end of most shifts during our changeover; especially later in the week when the banks had more money. Real armed robberies were happening all the time in the early 1980s – now they're a bit of a rarity.

I spent most of my time buying half-gram deals of heroin in Fitzroy Street, St Kilda. I would buy the heroin with one hand and put them in a headlock with the other. Literally. I loved those days. They moulded me as a copper and as a man. As Frank Sinatra said, 'If you can make it there you can make it anywhere.'

ONE Sunday morning, I was the watchhouse keeper. This means that you're in charge of the whole reception area and all the prisoners. You have to maintain the security, health and well-being of all prisoners as well as attend the watchhouse counter area.

At the time we had had a bit of a crackdown on the local street walkers, commonly known as 'crows'. So we had seven female prostitutes, three male drunks and a bloke on parking warrants in the cells.

The seven women were allowed to walk up and down the

whole walkway area, out of their cells. All the blokes were locked up in two cells. I started at 7am. At 7.05am I could hear the crows screaming out for cigarettes.

I opened the back door of the station and screamed at them to shut up. On doing this I noticed that one of them was holding up her t-shirt, exposing her rather large breasts.

This caused me to realise that smoking is not all that bad. I grabbed a packet of cigarettes from the prisoners' drawer and took the packet outside.

I found that after I handed the exposed breasts a cigarette, there were lots of other exposed breasts to give cigarettes to. Within an hour or so I would hear several girls screaming out 'watchhouse keeper, can I have a cigarette?' I looked outside and found all seven girls holding up their tops, pushing their breasts between the bars, screaming out for a smoke.

A short time later, Inspector Blaire walked into the watch house. Unfortunately, he was a deeply religious man. I was busy on the phone and he walked past me saying he was going to check the prisoners. I thought 'fine'. Then I realised too late that it wasn't fine at all.

I rushed out the back door to try to stop what was going to happen. It was too late.

He opened the door and walked towards the cells. Yep, you don't have to be told. They all lifted their tops, pushed their breasts through the bars and asked for a smoke.

Inspector Blair turned and looked at me. I looked at him, raising my eyebrows and smiling just a little in a desperate attempt to get him to see the funny side.

I truly believe he would have demoted me except for one thing – I was only a constable. It was in the days before you had to be politically correct. It was the crazy eighties; if that happened now you would be instantly dismissed and probably go to jail for extortion. I still think it was funny. On second thoughts, no, I don't.

WHILE working in undercover in St Kilda I found a new working girl, Sheree. She was a very large Maori with huge breasts. She was wearing a very short skimpy number and of course, like all of them, she was a heroin addict.

After speaking with her it became obvious that she was in fact a he. She said that she specialised in 'head jobs' to avoid embarrassing disclosures. My partner arrested her. We put her in the back of the van and drove her to the station. On entering the station we walked her past a policewoman called Jane.

Jane was the only policewoman on the shift so she volunteered to search Sheree. She could do it in the sergeant's office (as we could view the search through a gap in the curtains). Jane was very new in the job and very inexperienced. Sheree took her top off, exposing her large breasts, then she took her pants off. Jane could see something taped up to the inside of her left leg. Jane said loudly; 'What's that?'

Thinking that it was drugs. Jane called out, 'Angus, she's got something'.

My partner and I walked into the office. Jane pointed to the object. By this stage Sheree was undoing the tape. It wasn't only her boobs that were large – 'she' was a big-boned thing indeed. At this point a large penis fell down and hung between her legs. Jane screamed and said something about men in general and stormed out of the police station. As you can imagine transvestite prostitutes tape their penises back up between their legs to look and feel more feminine to the paying public. It was just another day in the office.

MARGARET was a chronic heroin addict who constantly swapped between street prostitution and house burglaries. One day, my partner, Darren, and I decided to check out who was staying at one of the cheap motels in Acland Street, St Kilda. It was always full of crooks.

As I entered the foyer I thought I saw Margaret enter a lift. I found the manager and asked him if I could see the 'booking in' file. I described Margaret and he told me he knew her by a different name. I asked him for the master keys and he gave them to me along with her room number.

I went upstairs without a warrant, of course. I always hated too much paperwork.

Darren and I listened at the door for a while. I could hear Margaret and some male talking about their latest crimes. We both entered, screaming, with guns drawn.

I put Margaret face down on the bed. When I entered the room she was standing over a small sink attempting to find a vein to inject a syringe that she had full of liquid heroin. The male was counting out cash on the bed. It didn't look good for them.

We handcuffed them both. There was stolen property piled up against the walls. On my radio I called for the divisional van to help take all the property and the crooks back to the station.

I picked up the syringe full of heroin and walked over to the sink and started to squirt it down the plug-hole, as we had enough evidence with the stolen property and the syringe was a health hazard for police.

Margaret didn't see it that way. She went absolutely berserk, screaming, 'What are you doing? Stop! How can you do that, you're wasting about $500 worth of somebody's property, you idiot.' She was serious. It was okay for her to steal property to buy the gear, but me getting rid of it was the crime of the century.

I WAS on the van in St Kilda when we found an elderly man in an old suit and tie. He was very drunk and abusive. He was sitting in a gutter abusing the world. I got out of the van and helped him to his feet. My partner grabbed him and started to drag him to the back of the van.

I told my partner to hang on a second. I asked the old guy how he was. He told me his best mate from the war had just died and he had been to the RSL for a few beers. He said it was his last mate in the world. He had none left. I asked him where he lived.

I helped him into the back of the van and put his seat belt on. I carefully started driving towards his home. My partner asked me where I was going. I said I was taking him home. My partner looked out the window, shaking his head. He wanted to take him back and put him in the cells.

I drove him home, got his keys and helped him into his home. My partner (an old senior constable) sat in the car. I undressed the old bloke and put him into bed. I referred to him as 'Digger'. I walked back out to the van and drove off. My partner said, 'You'll have to harden up if you're gunna stay in this job, mate.'

I just kept driving. I thought I won't stay in The Job if I have to harden up so much that I stick old soldiers in the cells for having a drink. Funny thing is, now I know he was right. You do have to 'harden up'. But there's no excuse for losing your compassion, and no value in it either.

chapter 3

THE GAME

'Even petty crims were prepared to brag if someone gave them the chance. I gave them that chance.'

THE Street was full of drug addicts who committed burglaries, stole cars and pulled armed robberies to support their habits. Then there were the street drug traffickers, their suppliers, prostitutes and, at times, their pimps.

It was the place that drew the desperate, the drugged, the lonely, the lazy and the mentally damaged. It was a different world and it had different rules.

I believed the game was ours and they were merely bit players. They would come and go, but we would remain.

When you got victims of an assault, robbery, burglary or whatever, you always did a computer crime check on them. A lot of the time the victim had more prior convictions than the crook. More than once we were called to a well-known thief's house and he'd be screaming because he had been burgled. He was actually very upset and appeared shattered, poor thing. He couldn't get insurance – it's hard to insure hot gear. No matter how hard I tried he could never see the funny side.

This environment attracted keen young cops. It was fast-track learning. In those days it was so busy that only the keenest of cops would go there. For me, there was an adventure around every corner. If there wasn't, I made one happen. My colleagues often said I could make the simplest arrest complicated. I think this was due to the fact that I always looked beyond the obvious.

I didn't just catch crooks – 'catching' sounds as if they blundered into my path. I hunted them. I hunted humans in the way a big game hunter stalked wildlife, except I had right on my side. They were not a protected species. Most of them were vermin.

Years ago I told someone that I hunted people. I remember thinking it sounded terrible, but it was true. I called my quarry the players. The players would just go about their daily routine. I would come along and make an adventure out of their misfortune (their arrest). At no stage did I ever take what I did lightly – I just tried to make it fun. I never looked at it as a job, more an extreme sport with the possibility of real bullets and real blood. The community paid me to do it. Amazing.

IN the early days after I'd been through all my training, I put in for St Kilda at the first opportunity. I arrived there in early 1985 and worked what we call general duties, which was everything from watchhouse duty, working in the car, working the divisional van, handling warrants and files and doing different jobs within the uniform section.

When I started, I'd decided I wanted to be the very best uniform member I could be. This would stand me in good stead to work plainclothes and one day become a detective. The idea was I would catch the snakes so I could go up the ladder. So away I went.

I immediately tried to catch every crook I could possibly find. I was a blue whale and they were krill – I would just scoop them up as I swam past.

I talked to burglars, prostitutes and all the 'drug-fucked scum bags' – as we referred to them – to try to cultivate them as informers.

Everybody wanted to do full-time plainclothes. It was the next best thing to being a detective, and incredible fun. I had worked in uniform, on the van and so on, for about twelve months when I was selected to work special duties, meaning full time plainclothes.

I lived and breathed to catch crooks. I was chosen to be the only full-time plainclothes member. Every two weeks another two members would come on with me and the three of us would work with one or two detectives from St Kilda CIB.

We worked the streets, or more correctly, one street – Fitzroy Street – mostly chasing drug traffickers. Then there were the burglars, armed robbers, theft from and theft of motor cars and various street offences. We would work anywhere there was a crime trend.

Very early on I teamed up with a person who is now my best friend, Darren. He was a few months senior to me and had the same aspiration – to become a detective as soon as possible.

He didn't show much enthusiasm toward working undercover, whereas I spent every minute of the day learning everything I could about the criminal sub-culture so I could just slip into it unnoticed.

The only way I could do that was to attempt to understand how crooks thought and how they worked so I could get inside their minds. I took the old saying about knowing your enemy to heart, and for me it was not easy. I had gone to a private school and had a sheltered upbringing in a nice, clean suburb. I certainly had no contact with criminals or criminal types or any contact with police. So this whole world was new to me. I was a tourist and, as a tourist, I tried to see as much as I could as quickly as I could before the novelty wore off.

I decided to make the most of every criminal I caught. When I caught a crook for anything – burglars, shop stealers, druggies, anything at all – I would do what I used to call 'suck on them like a lollipop,' to learn everything I could about their world.

In those days we had no taped interviews so you would have to sit down and type out every word – every question I asked and every answer they gave. I was, and still am, a one-finger typist, so typing took a long time. I didn't mind. It gave us time to talk.

EARLY on, I arrested a young women for shoplifting. She was a heroin addict with prior convictions for prostitution and I took her back to the St Kilda police station for questioning.

While I was interviewing her, she complained how slow I was at typing. She informed me that she had been a secretary (pre-heroin addiction) and could type eighty words a minute.

I thought that was great, so I asked her if we could swap seats. She sat with her back to the door and I sat opposite in the 'crook's' chair. I put my feet up on the desk, lit a smoke, leaned back and continued asking her questions while she typed them, followed by her own answers.

My partner laughed, thinking anything that saved time and effort had to be a good idea. The boss of the police station came into the interview room to check on the 'prisoner'. Bosses always have to do that. Anyway, the boss yelled and screamed at me for not following 'police procedure'. He wasn't a great lateral thinker. Looking back, I don't think he was a great thinker at all.

One-finger typing would cause you to interview them for hours. Back then, the law stated you could interview someone for no more than six hours and I can assure you, every single person I interviewed got the full six hours. That allowed me not to befriend, but to get close to, and build up a professional relationship with, these criminals. I was fascinated by their world and, because I was interested and not bored, many would open up and talk.

One thing I knew how to do before I started in The Job was to catch fish. I treated crooks just like I would fish. To catch a certain type of fish you would have to understand where they would be at certain times and why they would be there. That way you could use the right bait and tackle to catch them.

Being basically a pretty jovial and enthusiastic person, I was always cracking jokes with the crooks. Mostly they understood they were under arrest because they were idiots and had made some stupid mistake. They would sit there feeling sorry for themselves and I would try to boost them up and make them feel as though they were somebody.

I'd do that by getting them to let me into their world – I would talk about how they had committed their crime, where they committed it, why they used drugs, how they used drugs, how they interacted with their drug suppliers and other criminals. I found throughout my career that no matter how basic, stupid and drug-addicted these people were, they were proud of their achievements. Even the most petty crims were proud they were able to commit crime and were prepared to brag if someone gave them the chance. I always gave them that chance for my own reasons.

When I spoke to someone caught in a house doing a burglary, the last thing I wanted to do was talk to them about that burglary. There was no great need, because we had the offender red-handed. I would ask them where they'd slept the night before the burglary, what time they woke up, what they did when they woke up, where they went, which way they travelled from wherever they slept to where they were arrested doing the burg.

I wouldn't particularly want to know why they did that particular burglary. I wanted to know why they didn't burgle the hundreds of other houses they may have driven or walked past.

I wanted to suck their brains out. When I caught crooks, by the time I'd finished with them I had either driven them completely mad or built up a rapport. Sometimes both.

During the time of their arrest, I'd try to make them feel like they had something to offer, and it mostly worked a treat. I used to be fascinated at how they could steal a car and intrigued as to why some houses would be better to burgle than others.

Forget the no comment interview. I found that if you gave these criminals the chance to talk about what they did, they jumped at it. I did this purely so I could understand why they committed certain crimes, what attitudes they had towards police and other people. Most crims knew the routine in a police station and were easily bored. I tried to make the experience more fun for them by cracking gags and showing some genuine interest. That meant that many of them didn't mind me and opened up enough that I could learn from them.

One bloke I arrested showed me how he could open a locked door with a piece of string and a block of wax. I don't think I should explain how it works but, trust me, it works.

TAKE a good crook named Felix as an example. He was a top crook and once even made the Australian Top Ten Most Wanted list. Heroin brought him back to earth with a crunch – smack was a great leveller in the underworld.

I arrested him for a pissy armed robbery once. I remember trying to tell my partner that Felix had been one of the very best burglars around but he wouldn't believe me.

Working plainclothes one day, much later, I had a few beers with Felix and he told me how he used to work.

One day he dressed in a dark blue delivery man type shirt and pants. He purchased two bicycle reflectors and some double-sided tape then stood across the road from a large store in Chapel Street, Prahran, that sold video recorders, TVs and electronic gear.

He watched as the young shop assistant left the store to buy lunch. As he was leaving, you could see him take the lunch order from the shop manager. It was a lovely, warm day and the manager stood at the front door waiting for the next customer. He was only going to get one … Felix.

Our man grabbed his mobile phone and looked at the shop sign. On the sign was the shop telephone number. As he pushed the send button to dial the number, he began to walk a large industrial trolley across Chapel Street toward the door of the shop. As he got close to the store he could hear the shop phone ringing.

Felix left the trolley outside. The front door had the typical laser beam across the entrance which sounded a buzzer as a customer walked through the doorway. But Felix was no customer. He had stuck a bicycle reflector onto his pants just above and on the outside of each knee. The reflectors were at the right height to reflect the laser beam back onto itself. The reflector on his left leg allowed him to enter the store, the one on his right leg allowed him to leave silently.

As Felix entered the store, he jammed the mobile phone against his ear by lifting his shoulder. The manager's office was out of sight of the entrance to the store. Felix started to ask the manager about the price of TVs and video recorders while he picked up six boxes containing the latest state-of-the-art recorders, casually placing them on his trolley.

After putting twelve or more recorders and putting them on his trolley, he silently walked out of the store, pushing his trolley down Chapel Street. Once safe, he thanked the manager for his assistance and ended the call.

Felix was smooth, all right. Before he started using.

I ONCE arrested a bad-arse robber by the name of Shane O'Brien. He was a very fit bastard. When he was on the run, he was extremely desperate and dangerous.

What helped him become catchable was the fact that he became a junkie. When he was not a junkie he was untouchable.

I had spoken to him a lot, but I had not seen him for a

while. Anyway, I saw Shane walking out of the 'Caf' – the St Kilda Cafe. I called out to him as he was crossing the road. He looked at me, recognised me and sprinted straight across the road. I ran after him through the traffic in Fitzroy Street.

He headed for a car and dived head first through the open rear driver's side window. He did this running full bore. If it had been an Olympic event, he would have got a perfect ten from the judges. It looked as if the window was open for this exact reason.

The car was facing towards me. It took off, heading right past me and I knew I should let him go because I knew I would find him again, but I got caught up in the stupidity of the chase.

It had been raining. I grabbed the driver's side mirror and window frame.

The driver and Shane weren't in the mood to stop, even with a copper hanging on for grim death. They started accelerating up the street, dragging me along the road.

I was screaming at them to stop, I grabbed my handcuffs off a piece of elastic hanging on my shoulder holster and with them clenched in my fist I smashed the driver's window.

The glass shattered and I fell onto the roadway. Luckily I didn't go under the wheels and when I stood up I saw the local District Detective Inspector's car being driven by a constable.

I dived into their car (through the door, not the window) and we drove after them, but they lost us quickly as the DDI would not let us drive very fast, which was typical.

I soon found out that O'Brien was 'hot'. He was wanted on six apprehension warrants for burglaries, armed robberies and several car chases. I had taken the rego number of the vehicle and I was in a hurry to raid the house where the car was registered.

This was mainly because the owner of the car was a crook by the name of Andrew Dee who had just been released from prison and was on parole for an armed robbery he'd committed four years earlier.

My mentor, a very experienced detective sergeant in charge of me at the time, said it would be best to relax and let the crooks think that we didn't know the rego.

If we raid the home quickly, O'Brien would probably not be home. We had to play him like a fish.

Although O'Brien knew he was hot, he fronted at the Melbourne Motor Show. He managed to get into an office and stole the keys to a white Lotus sports car – the model used by James Bond at the time.

It was a Saturday and the big day for the show. The place was packed with people, but he calmly got into the Lotus, started it, drove it off a turntable and out of the building.

He had waited for the moment when someone opened a side door for a delivery or something. He drove the car around Melbourne, especially St Kilda, for a few days. Several car chases later he had to dump it and escape on foot.

After two weeks it was decided that it was time to raid the Doncaster address that had come up when we checked on Dee. By this time O'Brien would feel very safe. When we did a raid in those days there was no bullet proof vests, and no 'tabards' (vests with the word POLICE on them). We just raided the place flashing our badges.

About seven of us arrived at the address. It was about 5.30am and the kitchen light was on. You could see someone walking around inside as we crept up to the door. When we were all in position, the sledgehammer man looked at the sergeant and the sergeant nodded his head.

He lined up the deadlock on the door and brought the hammer back over his right shoulder. At that moment the door opened from the inside and there was Dee, dressed in overalls, carrying his lunch box and about to go to work.

Someone 'racked' a shotgun cartridge into a pump action shotgun about an inch from his nose. The metallic racking sound of this weapon is devastating when you're looking down the barrel from the wrong end. Dee instantly dropped to his knees and was placed face down, without a sound. He knew the routine. He was no fool.

Gun drawn, I entered the hallway followed by my partner Darren, while two of our team, Ross and Sandra, went toward the kitchen area.

None of us said a word until I located a female stepping out of a shower off the hallway. I screamed 'Police! Get Down.' I knew that shouting this out would alert O'Brien, but it had to be done.

A female police officer following us up the hallway immediately took over the custody of the female while I continued. I entered the next room and there was O'Brien just starting to sit up in bed, his eyes half closed with sleep.

I dragged him out of bed and put him on the floor. I handcuffed his hands behind his back. He was naked except for a pair of jocks. He was still muscular for an addict. I said something about how good we were. He just mumbled.

He was lying face down in the middle of the floor while we started searching under the bed and inside the cupboards. As the two of us were searching, I glanced over at O'Brien, who had sat up a bit. I abused him for disobeying my instructions and put him back face down on the floor. Forcefully. At this stage the other officers were searching the rest of the house. I was searching a large cupboard near the door of the bedroom and Darren was searching the drawers in the bedside table.

I heard something and glanced over my right shoulder to see O'Brien get into the sitting position. As I began to say, 'I told you …', he jumped to his feet and into the air, passing his handcuffs from behind his back under his feet to his front. It was a pretty good trick but I wasn't all that impressed at the time. As he landed I leaped towards him.

He smashed me in the chest with both of his hands clasped together, knocking me out of the doorway into Darren. As O'Brien sprinted out of the bedroom he grabbed a black beanie from a small table and ran into the hallway. I screamed, 'Stop!' but by this time it was more of a polite request than a demand. If I thought I was holding all the cards, then he had just produced another deck.

My yell caused Sandra to walk into the hallway and look toward our room. It was a bad move. O'Brien smashed her to the side of her head with both hands, sending her flying back.

As I got to the bedroom door, Darren and I crashed into each other, attempting to chase the nearly naked, handcuffed villain. At this stage O'Brien was almost at the front door. I screamed 'Stop him, he's getting away'. As I got to the door, O'Brien was well and truly out of the frontyard and running full bore up the street.

I chased him. As I got to the front gate O'Brien was just turning the corner out of the street, out of my sight. As I turned the corner about twenty metres behind him, I saw Ross. He was knocking the front of a large baton torch against the palm of his hand looking concerned and saying, 'Shit, I think he broke my torch, I think it's the bulb.' I could not see O'Brien anywhere.

I was annoyed that Ross still wasn't chasing the offender. I asked, 'Where is he?'

Ross said, 'It might just be that little flat wire thingummyjig is squashed and not touching the battery.'

I said, 'Where's O'Brien?'

Ross said, 'He's just over that fence. He's not going anywhere, now.' I looked over a small fence and there was O'Brien … out cold, lying face down on a rose bush.

Fortunately, our man had run to where we had parked our cars before the raid. Ross had gone to the car to get a torch to search inside the roof and was able to clock him. Both of them got their lights turned off, you could say.

Next second the police helicopter, Air 490, came screaming over the rooftops and started hovering above the light pole next to us.

The loud speaker bellowed 'Police, don't move. Lay down on the footpath and put your hands on your heads.' The whole scene must have looked pretty bad to the police helicopter crew as we all looked very scruffy and our cars were all unmarked.

I managed to show my badge to the pilot without getting shot. I picked up O'Brien's black beanie that he had grabbed on the way out of the house. There were keys to a stolen car he had parked around the corner, and a quantity of heroin.

To this day I have no doubt that if Ross wasn't 'Eveready', O'Brien would have made it to his stolen car and would have got away.

We would have been in big shit as there is nothing worse

than losing a crook. Especially a good one. Especially when he's been handcuffed, hasn't got any clothes on and there's four cops and one of him. We would have all been charged with negligence. It looks really bad on your record.

An ambulance soon fixed up O'Brien. We took him back to the station and interviewed him for numerous armed robberies, car thefts, escapes and all sorts of things. He was a good crook – but a sore one.

O'Brien got out about three or four years later and I recall seeing him in Smith Street, Fitzroy, while I was working as a detective. I was by myself, making inquiries over some other matter. We had a bit of a chat and a laugh about old times and I asked him to the pub for a beer, my shout. So we had a few beers. He explained to me how he'd gone in prison.

We spoke about one of the armed robberies he'd done and he described to me in great detail what an adrenalin rush he got from a job.

He'd done an armed robbery on a Commonwealth Bank in Kew. He and his partner were driving around with sawn-off shotguns. He described driving down the road and deciding that the time was right to do it.

It was right around the change of the police shift, about 3pm, midweek or something. He described looking at his partner and shaking hands as they do, a sort of overhand shake. They nodded to each other, meaning 'This is it – let's go.'

He described pulling on his balaclava, adrenalin pumping through him. He said he'd used most drugs in his life but none of them was as good as putting on a 'bala', jumping out of a car double-parked outside a bank, and running in.

He'd run in screaming at the bank tellers to try to frighten the living shit out of them. His mate was a big bloke and a bit too scary because when he started screaming for everyone to lie down, a couple of the women bank tellers were so scared they weren't actually listening to what he was saying. He had to push them down because they were just sort of frozen with fear.

O'Brien said he tried to scare the hell out of them so they treated him seriously, but not scare them so much that they were hypnotised. The truth was he scared the shit out of me. O'Brien didn't have to act tough and never did. He just was.

He was very proud that he had enough balls to do an armed robbery, would you believe. It was interesting to try and understand people like him because they seem to treat the risk of getting caught as we would treat paying tax. Jail was the tax they had to pay for robbing people, if they got caught. We were the tax collectors, and we all understood the rules.

That's the difference between them and us. As a detective, committing a crime such as a shop theft would be a massive risk. If I got caught I would lose my career and probably my family, the respect of all my friends and it would destroy everything I had.

But for a crim it is just part of the deal. They may not like jail time, but it is not the end of the world. So when we investigate a crime and think they wouldn't do that because they could get caught or 'surely they're not using their real name' or 'it's got to be a stolen vehicle', or 'they wouldn't have done it in their own patch', or other similar comments that detectives make, we suddenly realise we're not dealing with Lex Luther here. They are not master criminals, most of them. They're big, bad kids with guns.

Everything I heard first hand told me I had to stop thinking like a copper and think like a crook. We were dealing with criminals who live that way day to day. People often say incorrectly 'he's not a good crook he's got five pages of prior convictions.'

I believe that's wrong, because some of the very best crooks have five pages of prior convictions – but should have three hundred pages. They get caught and they learn and it makes a detective's job harder and harder each time they get caught.

Some learn the trade so well that although they may have been caught a few times when they were kids, the convictions dry up. It is not that they have gone straight, just that they have got smart.

chapter 4

NEVER BITE YOUR SERGEANT'S PASTIE

WHILE at St Kilda in the early stages, Darren and I watched a movie called *Supercop*. It was basically about two cops who join the force in New York and decide they're going to be detectives – and the best cops in the city.

One of their first jobs was directing traffic in the middle of New York. What they did, while off duty, but still carrying a badge, was to try their hand at working on drug dealers.

The movie was a true story, by the way – the opening sequence of this film shows the two detectives in real life – and we loved it. The movie had footage of one of the pair wearing a Batman T-shirt standing on a podium receiving valour awards for investigating and arresting massive drug dealers.

It cut back to when these two guys joined the police force and were best friends. They were catching so many crooks that they were eventually promoted. The movie ends with them on the podium getting these commendations. The good guys win and get the girl. Everyone lives happily ever after, except the crooks. Naturally, we thought that could be us.

We watched that movie several times and it looked good to

us. We decided we were going to be St Kilda's 'supercops'. We vowed that when we left St Kilda we would have made an impression on the community and the criminal class. We wanted to be feared by the criminals and, of course, respected by our superiors.

So we worked extremely hard and long hours. We did everything possible to cultivate informers and catch criminals. As it happened, we were quite successful. I don't know if we were as good as the two blokes from New York but we weren't bloody bad. And we did it without Hollywood scriptwriters helping us out of the tight spots.

I USED to go down The Street wearing this grey cotton jacket that I still have. Every time I went down there I wore it early in the shift. I'd walk the whole length of the street.

All the local crooks knew that every day there were plainclothes cops in the street who were either going to be on afternoon shift or morning shift. I made a point of wearing this jacket and walking from the top end of Fitzroy Street and sneaking around a little bit and pretending not to be too obvious, right down the length of Fitzroy Street. The word would soon be out that a plainclothes copper was sneaking about. Wearing a grey jacket, of course.

I'd then hide my jacket in the unmarked car, change my shirt and put on a different jacket, wear a cap and just completely change my clothing. I would then go in to try to sneak into a hotel or cafe and sit there for a while and let the street cool down.

One day it was great. Darren and I were having a drink in the Prince of Wales Hotel in the afternoon after walking the street in my grey jacket and then changing appearance. We were sitting at the bar having a beer. The barmaid was a transvestite who hadn't had the cut and tuck but had great big boobs and make-up all over the shop. She asked whether we lived locally and we said, 'Oh no, we're just travelling through.'

She just said, 'Well, be careful. There's an absolute prick of a copper out and about today. You'll know him, he's wearing this large cotton grey jacket.'

I asked, 'Who is he?'

She said, 'His name's Angus. Watch out – he's an absolute prick and he'll bust you for anything.'

So, we just sort of laughed. Afterwards, Darren punched me on the shoulder and said, 'You bastard.' I was really quite proud of being known enough to make it to the ears of the barmaid. I had a reputation, I had been noticed. It might not have been headlines but it was a start. Darren was quite jealous. We left the pub shortly afterward with Darren determined to receive similar notoriety.

Not long after we were both selected to be members of the District Support Group. We had an absolute ball. And they called it work.

This was about the end of 1986 and I was there for more than a year. Then I went through my exams and had enough arrest figures to attain the revered status of 'detective'. I became a qualified detective three years and ten months after joining the force, which was pretty quick, even in those days.

When I was training to become a detective, I had to 'do a board' and sit in front of three of my superiors. Everyone tended to have a very short haircut and turn up as though they had just left the academy. I'd had really long hair up until then, after eighteen months in plainclothes doing Special

Duties and District Support Group. I had to get it all shaved off back to a short back and sides, so I suddenly looked like the typical copper again.

But I still wanted to work undercover and looking like every other plod wasn't going to help. I went down and bought a wig, a long light brown one that went half way down my back. I then thought, 'How could I disguise my face?' So I used to fill my cheeks with toilet paper – tucking long rolled-up strips of it up under my upper and lower lips. That changed the whole shape of my face. It also changed my voice because I spoke with a lisp. Try it, you'll see what I mean.

I went and got an old green japara-type fishing jacket, stupid pants that were far too big, worn-out snow boots and a big floppy jumper under my jacket. I topped it off with an old canvas bag I used for fishing, which I filled up with empty bottles and rubbish. I would often stop and drink out of a half-empty cordial bottle which was about a two-litre size.

Every now and then I'd be walking down the street or wherever I was, and I'd open up my bag and pull out this massive cordial bottle and take a swig out of it. I really tried to look like the loser from hell – an absolute drop kick half a step away from lying in the gutter. Some would say it wasn't too hard.

I rubbed fat through my wig to make it look dirty, and the smell didn't do the disguise any harm either. Show me a dead-set street derelict and I'll show you someone you can smell from ten feet away. I found an old pair of square, thick clear glasses in a drawer of an old desk when I bought my first house.

When I put on the wig and the clothes I thought I looked

like a dog – a collie. So Dean Collie was born. I got all dressed up and into character and called Darren. I actually called him back to the office. I had been doing paperwork. Darren came in and wondered who the hell it was in the office. I showed him it was me. I asked, 'What do you think?' He thought it looked disgusting – in other words, it was sensational.

We thought we'd test it out on our sergeant. I went into the interview room and sat there on the wrong side of the interview table – the crook's side.

Darren rang up Angie, a policewoman who was with our sergeant, who was called Col. They were at Prahran picking up guns or something, and Darren called them back to the office. Darren told Col he'd just arrested an absolute loser trying to break into the police cars next to the DSG office.

This was a plainclothes office, with no police signs anywhere and all unmarked cars. Anyway, Darren explained away the fact I was missing by telling Col a porkie – that I'd had to go and pick up some paperwork or do some job that left him on his own.

Darren asked Col and Angie to come back quickly. When they arrived they marched straight into the interview room. Here I was, sitting at the table, the large fishing bag around my shoulder.

They looked at me dressed as Dean Collie and I couldn't see a flicker of recognition in their eyes, so I cringed away from them. Col said, 'Christ – what's in the bag?'

Darren said straight away, 'I got no idea. I haven't looked in it.'

Angie choked a bit at that one. 'You what?' she spluttered. 'You've arrested him and you haven't looked in that bag! He could have any bloody thing.' She went absolutely apeshit. Col gave Darren a disappointed look and said, 'For Christ's sake, get the bag off him and see what's in it.'

Darren said, 'I can't.' I started to enjoy myself and thought I had missed my calling and should have been an actor. I decided to start pushing the boundaries a bit.

I started screaming at them to leave me alone, saying, 'They're not your cars so why worry about it.' I was mumbling away. Col was eating a pastie and I jumped up and tried to grab a piece of his pastie.

Now, only a fool would get between Col and his late lunch. He stepped back, pulled his fist back just about to knock me out when Darren pushed me down in the seat and out of the punching line.

I sat back down again. I was keen on Col's pastie, but not a knuckle sandwich. I felt the chair start to fall, Angie stepped around in front of Darren and again started screaming to get the bloody bag off me to have a look in it, and I kept telling her that she wasn't going to look in my bag.

I watched Col to make sure that he didn't wind up a fair dinkum punch – I was enjoying myself, but I didn't want to end up with a wired jaw over a bit of fun.

I fell on my backside on the floor in the corner as the chair flipped. I reached across and pulled Angie's shoelace undone. Well, she's just screamed at the fact that I touched her.

Angie said, 'How dare you touch me.' She kicked me so hard you wouldn't believe, it took a heap of skin off my shin and just about dislocated my knee. I wasn't expecting it and I decided now was a good time to stop before she started to River Dance on my head. Not that I'd heard of River Dance at the time, but anyway.

With my right hand I brushed off my wig and glasses. I started spitting the toilet paper onto the floor, looked up at them. Angie completely lost it by this stage. 'This guy is a fucking lunatic! He's wearing a wig.' She went berserk.

Col was screaming to get the bag off me. But no-one seemed to notice that by this stage I had no disguise whatsoever. Angie shaped up to kick me again and I yelled, 'It's me, for Christ's sake. Relax, it's me.' I was backing up into the corner in real fear of receiving a beating.

It took them fair dinkum at least ten seconds to realise that they were actually looking at me. It was a long ten seconds because I was looking like a perfect candidate for an old-fashioned interview room flogging.

I looked at them and they just shook their heads in disbelief. I said, 'Now, do you reckon I could go down the street and buy some heroin?'

Col just shook his head and said, 'Angus, you could buy anything.' It did take them a little while to calm down because they were furious at me, and somewhat embarrassed. But then they all burst out laughing.

Dean Collie was born. He had passed the test and was allowed out in the public. I started to purchase a lot of small quantities of heroin.

What was funny was that I was able to buy heroin from traffickers that I'd already charged in the past. They knew me as Angus, but in this disguise they didn't recognise me.

You must remember that we weren't dealing with brain surgeons in Fitzroy Street – they were mostly drug addicts looking to score or rip someone off. And in any case, people everywhere see what they expect to see or what they want to see. Col and Angie had proved that. I stayed in dimly-lit spots on Fitzroy Street and I only ever came out at night. I could pick and choose. I would piss off the real dead-head street dealers and only buy and bust bigger dealers.

This worked really well until one bloke who I'd charged got bail. I was wired for sound so other cops were listening to what I was saying to these crooks. I had no high-tech equipment; I just carried a police radio in the back of my pants with an external microphone under my shirt.

I would push the radio button to transmit my conversation with the crooks to my partner. They could talk to me and tell me where they were, as I had a small ear piece covered by my hair. This wasn't state of the art but, hey, this was Fitzroy Street in its heyday.

I was wanting to buy heroin from a specific drug dealer. I had been after him for some time. Anyway, as I was trying to find him this drop kick of a dealer came up and wanted to sell me heroin. I said that I wasn't interested because I was waiting for someone and I knew their 'gear' (heroin) was top quality. This guy then became very abusive towards me.

He accused me of saying that his gear was shit. He then started threatening to punch my head in. He kept on and on trying to stand over me. Just when I would think I got rid of him he would be back.

He finally stated that if I didn't buy off him he would make sure I didn't buy off anyone. He then threatened to bash and rob me. He said something like this was 'his town'. How could this be? It was my town.

That was it. I decided to make his day and buy from him. I organised to buy off him in a side street that I knew we could cover. I did the deal, then slipped away to change. He was arrested – to put it mildly. Let's just say he hit the ground quite hard. Anyway, after we arrested him he learned the hard way he was in our town and he was just a tourist whose visa had run out. It is a sad world when you realise that you can't choose who you want to buy heroin from without being assaulted. Whatever happened to the customer always being right? Anyway, as it turned out, I was right … his heroin was nowhere near as good as my original target's.

IN those days we would specifically target any dealer who had the audacity to show off any wealth. If a dealer drove a sports car, wore expensive clothing or jewellery they were shitting in our face and soon regretted their vulgar displays of affluence, even if that came naturally to the sort of vermin who push heroin.

If they were waving a flag up and down The Street that said, 'I can beat the coppers,' they never lasted long.

I'd turn myself into Dean Collie once or twice a week. One night one of Dean's heroin trafficker victims who had got bail spotted me (as Dean) and got curious about certain things. In fact, he decided to interview me as to why he happened to get arrested seconds after selling me heroin.

The trouble was, he treated it like a real interview and started behaving like a real old-style detective. He started to attack me, and wouldn't take a backward step. At first it was verbally, then physically. He took to punching me in the head and kicking me.

I had a gun under my jacket, I had a large police radio tucked down the back of my pants and I had another tape recorder as well, plus all the other things. I had to be rescued by my cover crew. Then he was interviewed until he couldn't stand up. Various police to this day still comment on how funny it was to 'sit off' heroin traffickers selling heroin to 'Dean'. I used to say I was from Shepparton and I'd just come down because I'd just started using the 'gear'. I used to get a needle and constantly jab it in the same spot. I was going out with a nurse at the time who gave me this needle and I used to jab it in my arm and make what appeared to be a track mark. At times I would have to show my track to dealers.

A track mark is called just that because it is an exact needle mark that is used over and over again. It is used so much because it's an easy way to find the vein. It's used until that vein collapses due to it being polluted once or twice a day by powders that are allegedly heroin, speed or whatever, but usually have a lot of other shit in them that don't do the system much good.

To emulate the effects of drugs I would scratch my fake track mark and rub my eyes to make them red. I would even sniff water to try to give me a runny nose. All stuff that's indicative of heroin addicts. This allowed me to buy small quantities of heroin from street dealers without problems.

But nothing lasts forever and Dean had to retire for a while. But every now and again he was good for a comeback.

Later, when I was in the drug squad I would never pose as a heroin user. I graduated to being a drug supplier.

Users were to be spat upon and avoided at all costs. Heroin addicts in particular were dangerous. They were either planning to rob you or would lag you in to the police to get bail or cut down charges. There is nothing more dangerous to a drug trafficker than an addict.

I believe even cops come second.

chapter 5

A CUNNING PLAN

'I love it when everything goes like clockwork'

ONCE upon a time there was a team of the best, most enthusiastic, brightest and craziest young police officers from the big four police stations of St Kilda, Prahran, South Melbourne and Port Melbourne.

The members were all uniformed police who worked better out of uniform. In the old days they were called the Crime Cars, and then they went feral.

They were re-invented as District Support Groups and ours was called the Prahran DSG. Some of the funniest rogues and scallywags to ever don the blue discount suit passed through there. Gary Silk, who was later to be murdered in Moorabbin with Rod Miller, was an old Prahran DSG boy. He was a legend. They were great days.

I was selected as one the two St Kilda police representatives. I don't know if the bosses thought this was a promotion for me or if it was simply to get me out of their hair and make me someone else's problem.

We, of course, thought we were the best and the most experienced, as we were from the hardest and busiest station. All the other stations were only busy because they worked our borders. This is what we thought, anyway. To be honest, I still think it today, although St Kilda is not what it was in the late eighties, crime wise.

This period in my career was the ultimate in job satisfaction. I was doing plainclothes work in the best training ground Australia had to offer.

There were more drug traffickers, mostly heroin, per square inch than anywhere else in the southern hemisphere. At least, it seemed like it. I guess the cops in King's Cross and the red light district of Rio might reckon their patches have their moments, too.

It was a feeding frenzy. On top of all this, I was getting paid to do it. To catch crooks, that is. Catch them in the act, before the act, during the act or after the act. Many times, you were part of the act.

At times I had to pinch myself just to make sure it wasn't all a dream. I know police are supposed to be grim-faced when talking about the crime problem, but I'll let you into a secret that only other coppers know. This protecting the community stuff can be a hell of a lot fun.

I WENT to work one morning and found that no one really had any particular jobs to do that day – including me. I thought I would cook something up. The trouble was, the idea was only half baked when it popped out of my brain.

Over coffee in the main muster room I asked everyone if they could help me out on an arrest I wanted to make. The best part was that the boss was not in that day, so there were eight free plainclothes constables and senior constables to help me, with no bosses attached. The officer in charge of the plainclothes was only ever there to kick us up the arse when we stuffed up. Anyway, they all agreed to help, although some did roll their eyes and were obviously thinking 'What the hell am I getting myself into – again.'

I said, 'My briefing starts in two minutes in the conference room.' They rolled their eyes again … there was no conference room. This was it. The room we were in was our office, conference room, mess room and muster room. There were only two other rooms, the interview room and the toilet – and there was often shit in both of them.

With less than two minutes to spare I realised now was the time to come up with my plan. I knew from experience that whatever plan I made now would not even be remotely similar to the end result. But it is always good to have a plan.

From stuff-ups in the past I knew I could always refer back to the original plan when I hit the shit later. Hence the fact that the 'plan' always looks good – no matter what really eventuated.

The motley bunch of what appeared to be society's misfits sat before me waiting with bated breath. Make that baited breath – they smelled as if they had been eating worms. They were picking their noses, sitting with their feet on seats, smoking, playing with a basketball, and one kept shooting a small crossbow (seized exhibit) into an old dart board on the wall.

Joe was telling Ross that girls love a bloke who can touch his nose with his tongue. Paul had a small, thick circular rope with about a dozen different padlocks attached. He was practising with his 'pick lock set' – picking open one pad lock at a time. We all called him 'Harry' after Harry Houdini.

But believe it or not they were not the deadbeat losers they seemed. They were all hand picked, the best of the best. Each chosen from their station as the 'most likely to become a detective', each one hoping to be one of the few that ever make the CIB. You could look at this group and see which ones wanted to be undercover operatives, which ones wanted to be straight detectives and those heading for an institution for the criminally insane.

Undercover operatives always have this ridiculous over-the-top image of themselves – until they learn to just be themselves. They are far more effective if they drop the act and become real people, then work will follow and they will be the chosen ones. Chosen, that is, by their bosses to work undercover. But that was in the future.

I stood before them and waited for complete silence. It worked for Hitler when he stood before his half-mad troops. Eventually I said, 'I have received information that an unknown male driving an unknown vehicle is going to deliver an unknown quantity of heroin to an unknown male living in an unknown flat situated at number 147 Steven Street, St Kilda.'

Paul looks at the person next to him and says in a loud voice 'Thank Christ he knows something, this job was starting to look bad there for a while.' He was the station comic.

I pushed on, 'I also know the approximate time of the said delivery.' I didn't want to be appear unprepared.

Sandy said, 'Day time, night time?'

I said, '10am. Yesterday I was a long way off on the railway line and through binoculars I observed a male person walk to the public phone box outside the flats, ten minutes later a late model silver Ford Sedan arrived, registration unknown. A male, approximately thirty, brown hair, black leather jacket, wearing dark sunglasses, left his vehicle and walked into the flats. Three minutes later he was out of there. My information is that he does this daily.'

I sounded as if I knew what I was talking about so I continued. 'To effect the arrest obtaining the maximum amount of evidence I have devised the following cunning plan. Directly opposite this block of flats is a large park. I have arranged two large St Kilda Council trucks equipped with council uniforms, ride-on mowers, whipper snippers, branch cutters and rakes. If you have a preference for particular pieces of equipment, please see me after the briefing.'

All great leaders going into battle choose their own transport. Rommel, Montgomery, Douglas MacArthur and Guy Gibson VC couldn't all be wrong, and I wasn't going to be different. 'I will have the three-speed, four-stroke ride-on lawn mower,' I said, getting in before the rush.

Paul said, 'You're good at cutting people's grass.' Who said vaudeville was dead?

I then began to point to a sketch on the white board behind me.

'This is the park area. It is about the size of six house blocks. Our police vehicles will be left at the council offices.

'Paul, Dick, Ross and Louie – you will be in the two tonne open back garbage truck. Paul, you are in charge.

'Darren, Sandy (the only girl) and I will be in the equipment truck. Our job will be to effect the arrest of the drug supplier upon his arrival at the front of the flats. Paul, your crew is to execute a drug warrant on the flat of the buyer immediately upon the arrest of the supplier.

'Within the buyer's flat there should be evidence of large-scale drug trafficking. He is believed to be selling an ounce of pure heroin per day.'

The maths of drug dealing in the 1980s were simple and frightening. An ounce of pure heroin diluted with glucose down to five per cent pure made a pound of street quality. There are 453 grams to a pound and half grams were selling for $90 each. That equals 906 half grams at $90 each … a total of about $80,000 a day less the payment for the ounce of pure, which was about about twelve grand. That was a profit of about $68,000 tax-free per day. Now, in 2000, heroin is sold in major cities around Australia at around sixty per cent pure, and it is flooding in.

But that day we were just worried about catching this crew in the act. I told Paul: 'Within the flat there should be ample evidence of drug trafficking. There should be a minimum of over twelve thousand cash depending where he hides his profits, cutting agents such as glucodin sugar, a coffee grinder to cut and mix the rock heroin, and foils.'

'What we are looking for is evidence of unexplained wealth – cars, properties, gold and, of course, ostriches. For some reason drug dealers love buying ostriches. Anyway, at this stage are there any questions?'

Paul then decided he wanted to be a lecturer from detective training school when he grew up. 'How do you propose to identify the flat number and how do get a drug warrant for a flat when you don't know the number?'

I answered almost as though I had prepared for the question. 'I'm glad you asked that. Sandy, you are to, er, have a plan – I mean a pram. The pram that I am to get from, um, from the Alfred Hospital and you will be looking for a flat or something and will see the buyer go to the door of his flat, then I will write in the flat number ahead of the numbers 147, because I left a little space for that on the warrant.' Obviously I was making it up as I went along, and it was getting tiring. So I cut to the chase.

'Sorry, no more time for questions. Let's do it. We are all to be on channel 52. Good luck. Er, Ross, I know how you love gardening. Remember we're council workers. I don't want anyone working too hard out there. You'll blow our cover.'

So we drove down to the council office and picked up the two trucks containing all the equipment and council uniforms. I then got a short lecture from the boss in charge of all the equipment. The boss insisted that we keep working whilst in council uniform as he didn't want any complaints. I assured him that all would be okay, and we wouldn't tarnish the reputation of his outdoor staff who, as far as I knew, weren't exactly famous for setting any records in the manual labour department. I was always an optimist, and actually almost believed myself when I solemnly told him we'd keep up the good work against weeds and litter.

I drove the front truck and parked in the middle of the park. I acted as foreman, directing who was to do what. Just before arriving in the street, I dropped Sandy off.

Sandy was dressed in a tight-fitting tee shirt and jeans. I had managed to get a practice resuscitation doll as a baby to go with the pram from the local hospital.

Nothing ever costs a thing. When you're a plainclothes cop appealing for assistance people always help out. I always promise to tell them how the whole job finishes up. This is so they have a story to tell during their next dinner party.

Anyway, we all made jokes about who the baby looked

like. We all had a great laugh. Sandy embraced the role (and thought it was very funny) although she didn't seem to me to be quite the baby type. More the babe type.

So there we were. We unloaded the gear, and got started. I was driving the ride-on mower. Paul saw a large branch on a large gum tree and decided that it better be cut down before it fell on somebody's head. In other words, he wanted to use the chainsaw because we had one.

Sandy walked around the park pushing her pram. The most difficult part of her job was to avoid nosy mothers wanting to look at her baby. We got there around 9am. I asked Sandy when she was going to breastfeed. She just gave me a look that said, 'Not in your life time.'

At 10am I had finished driving around the park and had no more lawn to mow. So I dropped the blade down a bit and started to mow the park again. I gave it a Number One cut, shorter than a first week recruit at the academy. We were all starting to get bored when I suddenly saw the buyer walk out of the flats. I indicated to the others that it was him.

Sandy started to walk over to the front of the flats. This male had a good look at us and walked to the public phone box. He made a call and returned to the flats. Our main dealer should arrive with the heroin soon, according to our cunning plan.

As he was walking back to his flat, Sandy cut him off and asked him where an old girlfriend of hers might live. This buyer was happy to talk and started to tell her who lived in what flat. The end result was that while Sandy was knocking on another door she saw him enter flat seven. Her job was over. She walked back and said, 'Seven.'

I then gave Paul the flat number and he informed his crew.

I told everyone that we were right to go. In about ten minutes our target should arrive.

I grabbed a football out of my bag in the truck and we all started to play kick to kick. All except Sandy, of course. We were having a great time up until the local busybody decided she was going to act on behalf of all the ratepayers. She walked up to our group and demanded to speak to the boss. They pointed to me, which was generous of them. I walked up to her. At this moment we were standing in between the two trucks in the front of the park.

She abused me for wasting the ratepayers' money – words to the effect of 'I been watching you and your men for over an hour and you've done nothing. You're all poncing about wasting time and now you're playing football! What's your name? I'm reporting your behaviour.'

I said, 'I am Senior Council Worker Bartholomew Aardvark.'

At that moment a large silver Ford Sedan started turning into our street, driving straight toward our position. I then said in a loud voice, 'Okay, everyone. I want you all to get back to work now.'

My crew all got the message, looking at the silver Ford drive slowly toward us. We all walked to the rear of our trucks, but Mrs Windbag followed and said, 'Not before time. You haven't gone near the play area – there's rubbish everywhere.'

The silver Ford stopped just past the flats. As the driver stepped out of his vehicle Paul pulled out a sledge hammer from under rubbish, the others removed shotguns. They loaded, then strode across the road like the *Texas Rangers,* or maybe like the *Super Mario Brothers.*

I removed my .38 revolver from its shoulder holster and held it down by my side. Mrs Windbag just looked at us with her mouth open. She walked slowly away – backwards. It was a good move. I was getting tired of her.

Sandy casually reached down and removed a .38 revolver from beneath the baby doll in her pram. Darren, Sandy and I walked ahead up behind the male as he walked onto the footpath. I tripped and pushed him face first onto the concrete foot path next to a low brick fence.

The other two covered me from any danger that might come from the target or from behind. Within a couple of seconds he was cuffed, then began whinging and complaining, but you don't worry about a crook sooking up when you are on a raid. I would have given him something to complain about but we were a little busy to get involved with gratuitous violence at that stage.

I then heard the sound of crunching and crashing as flat seven was breached. There was the faint shouting of 'Police. Don't move!' I knew the job was right.

Then there was that terrible silent pause, that massive let down as you realise the arrest doesn't live up to the excitement leading up to it.

During that pause I looked up the street. I saw a large silver Ford Sedan commence a right hand turn into the street. I looked up at Darren and said, 'Quick, drop your gun alongside your leg. Sandy, kneel down and pretend you're helping this bloke'. This job was not over and maybe there was still fun to be had.

I looked down at my prisoner. His leather jacket was not leather. It was vinyl, and the sun glasses were cheap. As an insurance policy I whispered into this bloke's ear: 'Where do you live?' He stuttered, 'Fla-, Fla-, Fla-, Flat 2/147 S-s-s-s-steven Street, h-h-here.'

I turned my head slowly and channelled myself towards this new silver Ford driver. As I walked over to the roadway I could see that this driver matched everything I was looking for. I started to limp onto the road in front of the Ford. The driver was madly looking around trying to sum up the confusion before him.

We were all still wearing council safety jackets and council pants. I screamed out, 'There's been an accident Help, Help.' As I got to the driver's door I slipped out my .38 and pointed it at his head. As I did this Darren positioned himself in the best place for someone with a shotgun – the bonnet.

Darren pressed the shotgun against the windscreen at the driver's head – it really does get their attention. All the target could see was the barrel of the gun a few inches from his face. It must have looked like a bazooka at that range. He froze and stopped the car. He was no dummy.

I dragged him out the open driver's side window onto the roadway. I started to search him. Nothing. Then I pulled off his big high cowboy boots and a white rock the size of a golf ball wrapped in clear plastic fell out of his boot.

I called out something obvious like, 'It's him' or 'got him'.

Darren mumbled something like, 'Thank Christ for that.'

I stated a great rule of policing at that moment: 'The more people you arrest the more chance you've got of getting it right.' Eventually.

Then I let myself hear the first 'arrestee'. He was bleating about the whole situation. I walked up to him and thanked him warmly for assisting us arrest a big heroin dealer. At that moment Paul walked up, stating that there was a shitload of evidence in flat seven – $50,000 cash, scales, glucodin for cutting the heroin.

I was uncuffing the innocent man when Paul said something like, 'Hey cockhead, what's your name?' He could have been in public relations if he hadn't been a copper.

I said, 'Oh no, this gentleman helped us arrest that heroin dealer. Without his help we would have nothing. On behalf of the Victorian Police Force, the Chief Commissioner himself and the people of this fair state, I would like to thank you, sir.'

He opened his mouth several times as though he was going to say something but nothing came out. He looked like a fish out of water.

I stood the bloke up and brushed him down just like 'Maxwell Smart' would do. He was pleased to be alive and he thought being free was good too.

So he left. Well he didn't just leave, he sort of ran, tripping over twice at he went. There were no complaints though – I don't know why.

I parked his car properly as he ran into the distance. After all, they call that customer service. Later on, as we were leaving I saw him peeping around the corner to make sure we were gone before he returned home.

I was on a high at finally catching our target – I love it when everything goes like clockwork.

While Darren had the crook I started to search the brand new silver Ford Ghia sedan. While I searched it, the alarm went off. Darren asked the crook, let's call him Rudi, how to turn it off. Rudi stated that he needed to push the code into the code pad. I had a better idea and said, 'What, this one?' and ripped it out of the dashboard and then tossed it to him with a wire hanging out of it. It landed quite near Rudi's head.

I disconnected the battery but the alarm continued because it had its own hidden battery. When we stripped the car we found $15,000 in cash hidden under the centre console. The drugs and money were photographed and placed in an exhibit log, naturally.

Moments later Paul arrived with his man. We took him (our prize) back to the station. I sat with him in the back seat of our vehicle while we drove. He didn't seem to be enjoying the trip.

I said to Darren, who was driving, 'Do you know what I hate most about drug traffickers?'

He said, 'They're blood sucking leeches?'

'No.'

'They're dirty, rotten filthy maggots that live off the misery of others, and lower than mouse shit.'

I said, 'Close, but no.'

Darren said, 'They smell?' He was getting desperate.

I then looked at Rudi straight in the face and said through my teeth, 'They don't pay tax.'

I then elbowed Rudi in the chest. It hurt him, causing him to bend forward.

I then whispered into his ear, 'Tax time.'

Darren thought about it and said, 'You're right, Angus, I hate that!' It was as though he had just realised that drug traffickers don't pay tax.

We interviewed them, remanded them in custody and went to the pub to celebrate. It was a great pinch.

Drug dealers doing business or just interacting with their families are well dressed, arrogant, confident, smooth, standing tall with their shoulders back, and always 'cashed up'.

Money is power and they are loaded. They don't have to go to work every day or struggle to pay the mortgage. They want something, they buy it. Even some people who know what they do, somehow don't mind because, in a twisted way, they appear 'successful'.

But as soon as the cops catch them, they turn into slimy little insignificant weeds that can't even look in the mirror. No-one wants to know them. They drop their shoulders and lower their heads. They don't even like themselves. We remind them at every opportunity that they are bottom dwellers.

chapter 6

THREE LITTLE PIGS

'You should have opened the door'

I WAS driving down the road with Darren one morning when we were working at the St Kilda District Support Group plainclothes office.

We were stopped at a set of traffic lights when I noticed the strong smell of marijuana. I traced the smell to an old Holden station wagon upwind from our position. We pulled it over. I told the driver he had a big problem as it was only 8.15am and he was already smoking dope.

The bloke was stoned off his head but still managed to drive. I pulled him over. The only grass he had left was in his joint. We searched and found nothing.

While we were talking and searching I got into the front seat and made myself comfortable. I lit up a normal smoke. Darren jumped in the back and put his feet up. It was peak-hour traffic and we needed a break.

It was obvious to anyone that we didn't want to bust him. I asked the bloke if he could tell us who his supplier was. He tried to put on a serious face and explain to me that he was not an informer. He was not a brain surgeon either.

I decided I would take another approach.

I said, 'Listen mate, as you know I'm an undercover cop. We both are. Now I'm going to have to trust you.' I looked over my shoulders to make sure no-one was listening and said, 'I'm a choof head myself. Have you got any idea how hard it is to "get on" (buy grass) when you're an undercover cop? No-one wants to know ya.'

He said, 'What a bummer, man. No-one would like ya. Bummer.'

I said, 'I just want a choof, man, that's all I want. I don't want to bust people.'

He said, 'That's right, man, wake up in the morning and you're a nark. That's heavy shit, man. That's bad shit. You need a choof, I need a choof, hey.'

I said, 'Can you help me get some choof?'

He said, 'Yeah man, but I'm empty. Be nice to people, you need to mellow out. We better take my car, Ted knows my car.'

I said, 'I'll drive.' Then I added as an afterthought, 'Not that I don't trust ya.'

I pulled over and became Dean Collie. Choofhead could not believe his eyes. The average Angus became the classic doped out 'drop kick' Dean.

Choofhead had those far away eyes of a heavy dope user. His eyes kept closing, his head kept swaying around as though it didn't know where it should be. I drove, it was much safer. He then directed us to drive back in the direction he had just come. After a short drive he told me to pull over.

He said, 'Take the keys out.'

I took the keys out of the ignition. He took them from me. He said, 'See this key ring, it has the map of Australia on it. See the letters B.B.B.A.C and a little marijuana leaf in the middle of Australia? Well this is the key to the Be, Buy, Back, Australian Club It means, "Be Australian, Buy Australian and put it back into Australia Club." Cool eh? Ted thought of that.

'Now, all you have to do is come with me into that house right there and pay $20, and you're on. Ted will then give you the medallion and you can buy gear whenever you want between 9am and 5pm Monday to Friday. He has weekends off. Come in and meet Ted.'

I had no idea who Ted was or who was in the house. I said, 'Here's $20 for the medallion and $20 to buy me a "G" (gram).'

I walked with him to the house. There was a large security door that blocked off the verandah. Choofhead rang a bell and a man appeared through the front door. They exchanged money for drugs through a small spring loaded letter vent situated in the middle of the security door.

We then returned to the car and drove off. He was very happy with himself. He asked me if he could have some of the purchase. I refused, stating that I needed it more than him – which was quite true, as far as it went. I needed it for evidence. He reluctantly agreed. Then again, he had no choice. Darren and I drove Choofhead's car back to ours and said goodbye.

As two baby Supercops we were quite happy with ourselves. We drove back to the station and made all the usual checks on the address, electricity, rates, telephones and such. We found that the house was supposed to be a centre for wayward youths and the operator was a bloke, Edward (Ted) Smead, who had two prior convictions for possessing small amounts of marijuana.

A check of Smead's bank records revealed he had large

amounts of money in several accounts and was recorded as being involved in the import-export trade.

It was all coming together beautifully. We started the day having a chat with a choofhead and we would end it with a major bust.

We planned to raid the house later that afternoon, having obtained a search warrant issued under the Drugs Act based on Dean's observations of the drug purchase. We sent another couple of cops to go down and 'sit off' the house while we set up for the raid.

Those members contacted us a short time later. They'd seen several customers buying grass from the house every few minutes, and most of them were in their teens.

I decided to raid the house at 4pm as there would most likely be the best evidence. I guessed Ted wouldn't have been able to bank the money and he would still have some drugs in the house.

At the office I gave members their duties. I informed everyone that there were no problems expected as it was a normal house in a suburban street in East St Kilda.

I hand-picked the team for special duties – the biggest one got the sledgehammer, and the second biggest got the crowbar.

We had the crowbar to force open the security door and once it was open the sledgehammer would force open the front door.

I directed one crew to intercept a drug purchaser as he left the house. Once one was arrested I would give the signal to go. I was confident it would be a text-book raid.

We drove and parked not far away. When a radio call came that one of the dope buyers had been arrested away from the premises, I gave the signal. We parked our cars just down from the address and walked up to the house in a line – a bit like the *Texas Rangers*. The crowbar man was first, followed by the sledgehammer man, followed by me and four others.

As we stopped at the security door, two members walked to the back of the house to cut off any escape. Any person watching would have known we had obviously rehearsed our roles.

I looked at crowbar man and nodded. He then started to jemmy open the security door. He pushed the bar into a crack in between the door and its steel frame. He tried and tried but could not get the jaws of the jemmy deep enough into the crack.

After scratching away for what seemed forever I indicated to him to fall back and, defeated, he moved out of the way. I then nodded to the sledge hammer man on the tried and true belief that when science failed always use dumb force. He walked forward and measured where he was to strike.

Smash … smash … smash.

You could see him vibrate as each blow struck solid steel. It was now very obvious to anyone within one hundred metres what we were doing and I started screaming 'Police, police, don't move.'

The door was about to give way any second and we were already to burst in once it splintered. You could see the hammer man was getting angry at the door for not giving way.

Smash … smash … smash. Each smash was getting harder but then each blow started to get weaker. I then grabbed the hammer off him. He bent down gasping for air, as it was very hard work. I started to smash.

The front door inside the security door opened. Ted looked at us as if we were a pack of encyclopedia salesman. He casually said, 'What's your problem? Piss off.' Ted seemed to know something we didn't.

I said, 'Open the door now.'

Smash … smash … smash went the hammer.

Ted called out, 'You're scratching the paintwork, now piss off.' I was beginning to develop an intense dislike of Ted.

I then bent over gasping for air. One of the other troops came back and said, 'I've been all around the house, all the windows have heavy steel bars and the back door looks even stronger.'

I then asked the next bloke to start hitting the security door. Away he went, swinging like Jack O'Toole from the backmark on the *World of Sport* woodchop, but without the same results.

I had to admit defeat. There was no way we were going to get through this solid steel security door, let alone the front door. If Hitler's bunker had been as well made he wouldn't have had to top himself. He would have starved to death before the Russians got in.

The occupants inside the house started laughing away. I heard a female voice say out loud, 'Ted, I think there is someone at the door.' They all started laughing. I felt like the big bad wolf outside the house of bricks. The cops around me then started yelling abuse – I don't know if it was at Ted or me. This was a very bad situation.

The first thing that hit me was the fact that I had never heard of police not being able to get into a house. This one was a complete fortress.

Kids kept coming to the house to purchase. They would

then see us and disappear. Then it started. Darren and the rest of the troops started stirring me. 'Got any more bright ideas, Elliot Ness? Um, what was it? No problems expected, an ordinary suburban house.'

They all started to blame me for their embarrassment. I had no come back as I had not conducted any reconnaissance to check the target's security. I had taken it for granted that it was a normal house security door.

The front door opened. It was our Ted carrying a phone. He brought the phone to the security door and said, 'Here you are, my solicitor wants to talk to the boss. Is that you?'

He passed the phone through the letter slot. I put down the sledgehammer and took the phone. I had to bend down a bit to get the phone to my ear. I said, 'Hello, yes. This is Acting Sergeant Angus of the "I" District Support Group. Yes, yes, I can appreciate that but … yes, yes, I know your client has rights. Yes, but we have a warrant to search … drugs, yes. Well, he might want to make no comment but first he must let us in. Yes, okay, bye.'

I looked at Ted. He was standing about a foot from my face, within the security of his fortress. Smiling. It was a big smile. He made sure he smiled at all of us individually. He gave the biggest smile to me. I wanted to punch that smile right off his face.

He raised his eyebrows as though he wanted me to talk to him. I refused. I said, 'Come on, everyone, let's go.' I heard one of the crew say behind me, 'But.' I said, 'Let's go.'

We all left. We arrived like *Texas Rangers* and left like Brown's cows.

Ted called out, 'Bye, see you later. Come back soon.' Did I mention that I didn't like him?

Embarrassed was not the word. Personally embarrassed, professionally embarrassed, and emotionally embarrassed. We got back to the office with our tails between our legs.

As we walked in the front door, the boss said to me, 'What is going on? I've just had two newspapers on the phone to me about you harassing a youth drop-in centre in East St Kilda.'

I told him what happened. He said, 'What do you mean you couldn't get in? What are you, a pack of Avon ladies? I've never heard of cops not being able to get in.'

I said, 'Have now.'

This was juicy gossip, and I was the subject of it. The next day everyone in the entire police force knew that I had led the charge on a house and couldn't get in.

I conducted surveillance on the house again. The day after the failed raid he was back trafficking full bore with kids buying grass flat out through the front security door.

Ted would leave the house now and then but I didn't want him without the evidence within his home. Someone always remained in the house so he never had to carry keys with him when he left to buy smokes or something. I knew that because I had him searched. Nothing.

We all went out to the pub to commiserate and Darren and I had a ten-pot conference as to what we were to do next. We spoke about how Ted had gone to the media to try to stop us having another go.

He claimed we were persecuting him and that all he wanted to do was to help and support wayward youth. I still had a search warrant that was 'unexecuted.' I needed to rectify this situation – and quickly.

We needed the heavyweights and so we called in the boys who won't take no for an answer – The Special Operations

Group. They were briefed and were keen to pop in on Ted to say hello. Our motley crew were told to wait near the address until the SOG had done their thing. We were not to get in the way.

One of them went deftly into the frontyard, climbed the side fence and jumped onto the roof of the house. He then quietly removed four tiles and stood there.

He then signalled he was ready. He was to enter through the roof once we had breached the front door. Meanwhile another Soggie dug a hole down next to the toilet down pipe.

He then got ready to hit the pipe with an axe. Once the attempted entry began it was his job to cut the toilet down pipe and catch any drugs that the crooks may try and flush.

When they were ready the SOG turned up with their four-ton front door key, a specially designed crash truck.

One jumped out, grabbed a hook attached to a heavy chain from the rear of the truck and ran up to the security grille. Another ran up to the security grille and hit it twice with a large axe. The axe made a small hole in the grille right next to the main support. He placed the hook through the hole and around the main support. One then yelled, 'Clear, go!'

The chain took up the slack, the hook wrenched at the front grille area. The wheels spun. They reversed, right back until they hit a small low brick fence. The fence fell over. The single-fronted California bungalow held firm.

They accelerated full bore, this time with feeling. The chain was as tight as it could be without breaking, then the security grille gave way. It was attached to the cement and brick veranda and the veranda was attached to the front of the house. The front of the house was attached to the roof and both walls.

The whole front of the house came off and crashed onto the front garden. One copper on the roof fell off with a scream and fell harmlessly into a large bush. They breed them tough. It was a rose bush.

And I'd thought we were only going to pull the front security grille off to let the sledgehammer man try to smash the front door down.

But now I could see right through the house. Several troops ran into the house, grabbing the three occupants. Someone yelled to get out quickly.

As they staggered out the whole house started to collapse and, as they ran clear, the unsupported walls gave way under the weight of the roof. Moments later the whole house caved in with a crash.

I looked on in disbelief at the carnage and mayhem. Ted stood about three metres in front of me, handcuffed. Through the wreckage you could hear Ted's phone ringing. He was covered in white plaster. His face was one of shock and terror.

So was mine.

But as he looked at me I recalled the face he was wearing when he had smiled at me when we couldn't get in the first time. And my face took on the same sort of smirk.

I then gave each of the arrested occupants the same smile, individually wrapped for their enjoyment. I saved the biggest smile for Ted. I raised my eyebrows at Ted, expecting him to say something. He didn't. There was nothing to say.

Actions, as the saying goes, speak louder than words. It had taken a little while, but we had acted.

I stepped forward and tucked a copy of the search warrant into the front of his shirt. As I tucked it in I said, 'You should have opened the door.' I started to walk away. I looked at the wreckage, stopped, smiled, turned around and said slowly, 'No, on second thoughts, you shouldn't have.'

WHEN we searched the remains of the house, we found three small gram packets of grass.

Locating any drugs at all, even a little bit of grass, meant that the raid was justified and the cost of all damages was the responsibility of the owner and not the responsibility of the police force.

Many a beer has been drunk re-living this raid. I maintained we used 'reasonable force'. You're not supposed to 'shoot flies with shotguns,' as they say, but we did have the failed raid behind us to back the use of more serious force.

When the magistrate found Ted guilty of possessing and trafficking marijuana, he ordered he be placed on a good behaviour bond for twelve months.

The magistrate was aware of the failed raid. He had also seen photographs of the house after the warrant was marked 'Executed'. The magistrate frowned at me. He then gave me a small smile and left the court.

After the magistrate was out of sight I started to walk out. The clerk of courts walked up to me and said, 'Mr Angus, the magistrate asked me to inform you that your job is to bring them before the court and he is the one that decides the penalty, not you.'

I shrugged. The clerk added, 'He said, "That Angus is never going to die wondering is he? Tell him to keep up the good work".'

I said, 'Thanks. Can you tell him that I really just wanted to remove the front security door, but the door was connected to the verandah and the verandah was connected to the wall, and the … anyway.'

The house itself was insured for $110,000 … but not against police acting on a lawful warrant. No insurance. Ted lost the lot.

That was the end of the 'BE, BUY, BACK AUSTRALIAN CLUB.'

chapter 7

A CRUEL BARB

'The dog thought it was Christmas. His very own person to eat'

DARREN and I were working The Street in plain clothes when a call came over the radio of 'Offenders On'. The call stated that a neighbour had seen someone break into a house across the road in a side street. We decided to run there as it was only around the corner.

We got to the house and were the first coppers to arrive. I notified D24 that two plainclothes members were at the scene. I ran up to the front door and Darren ran around the back to cover the rear.

I knocked on the front door and found it was open. A man about thirty years old walked out of a bedroom into the hallway. I had obviously startled him.

I said, 'Hello, I'm Constable Angus. We had a report that someone had broken into this house.' I showed him my police badge and asked, 'Have you seen anyone?' He looked shocked and said, 'No, I am the owner and if someone came in I would know.'

Two marked police cars then stopped at the front of the house.

I said, 'Sorry to bother you, sir.'

I then called out to Darren that everything was fine. I stopped and turned back to the owner who had just started to walk back into the hallway.

I said, 'Excuse me, sir, may I have your name for our sheet.'

He said, 'Raymond Collins ' and closed the front door.

Darren walked back into the frontyard. I waved to the uniform cops that everything was all right. They got into their cars, as one member was getting in he called out, 'Are you going to reply to D24?'

I said, 'Yeah.'

I spoke into my portable police radio, 'DSG 300 to VKC.'

D24 replied, 'VKC to DSG 300, go ahead.'

I said, 'Your last at 17 Lord Street, St Kilda, all okay, N.O.D.' ('No offence detected.')

I walked out the front gate, stopped as though it was an afterthought, opened the letter box and grabbed three letters. They were all addressed 'Mr Stephen Frederick'. This was not good.

Darren had walked out of the yard onto the street. He stopped and looked back at me. I said, 'It's him.' Those words set off a sudden sound of running steps inside the house. I said, 'He saw me check the letter box.'

We both ran around the side of the house to the back yard just in time to see him jumping the back fence. I was ahead of Darren.

We chased him through several houses, crashing full bore into fences. I was doing well until I jumped a fence straight into a large wire clothes line that was attached to the other side of the fence. It acted like a net – the more I struggled the worse I was tangled. As I was struggling, I heard Darren get bailed up by a big dog. I had already run through that yard but that must have just woken up the old dog when Darren jumped into his patch.

The dog decided that his only bit of space in the world was not going to be used as a thoroughfare. The dog thought it was Christmas. His very own person to eat.

As I was still half suspended above the ground, upside down on the clothesline I heard a very loud scream of pain. It was so loud that even the dog stopped attacking Darren for a moment. I called out, 'Stop playing with the dog and catch that bastard.'

Darren said, 'I can't shoot a Shepherd.'

I got out of the clothes line and peeped back over the fence. My partner was hanging upside down from a low branch of a gum tree. The German Shepherd was jumping up trying to bite him. Meanwhile the terrible screaming continued. It wasn't Darren. As he looked relatively safe, providing he didn't drop from the tree, I decided to continue the chase. I jumped over two more fences and found the source of the screaming. By now it was more like an agonised whimper.

Before me was our burglar. There was a two-metre high wrought iron fence that ran along the side of an old large Victorian home. The fence was made from large vertical wrought iron bars about four inches apart. At the top of each bar was a thick moulded steel arrow head.

The arrow heads were meant to be blunt, but the fact that the owner of the house had run an angle grinder over each one and made them sharp. The top of each bar was now sharp – and rusty.

Our burglar had run up to the fence and placed the middle of his right palm on top of the arrow head. In his haste he had put all his weight on it, the arrow head had pushed through the fine bone and flesh exiting the back of his hand. He and the fence had become one.

He was standing on his tip toes in an attempt to take the weight off his right hand, his eyes were closed, his head back.

As I ran up to him I swiftly whipped my hand cuffs from a strap on my shoulder holster, grabbed his free left hand and hand-cuffed it to the iron fence. Then I proudly pronounced, 'Gotcha. You're not obliged to say or do anything and all that shit. You understand?' He said through the pain, 'You're sick.'

I turned and screamed out, 'Darren, I got him.' The crook managed to whisper, 'You didn't get me, you arsehole.' I really didn't care if he wanted to argue semantics. I was happy with the result. He wasn't.

Several uniform members then arrived. They all laughed, of course. We were all laughing. Some of the coppers were wincing at the thought of all that pain, but then again he was just a burglar. I explained to all the new arrivals that I had caught him. Among other things, the crook kept saying was 'You didn't catch me.' He didn't get the joke.

I grabbed a portable radio and called for an ambulance. The radio operator said, 'Is it a member or the offender, and what is the injury?'

I said, 'It's not serious, the offender has hurt himself.'

The offender seemed to disagree. 'Not serious! Hurt himself! HELP ME!'

It was funny because the crook started to call out for other people, members of the public, to come and help him. For some reason he didn't have confidence in the police members present. It was an insult. One of the uniform police stepped forward and offered him a bullet to bite on. Again everyone laughed – except the skewered suspect.

Me as a fresh-faced copper at my graduation, mid-1984.

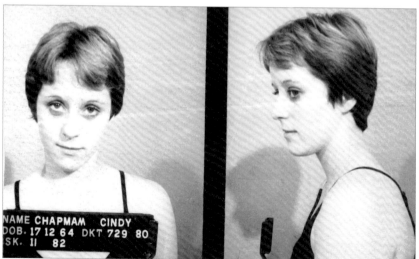

The needle and the damage done ... four faces of Cindy on a one-way trip.

NAME CHAPMAN SINDY

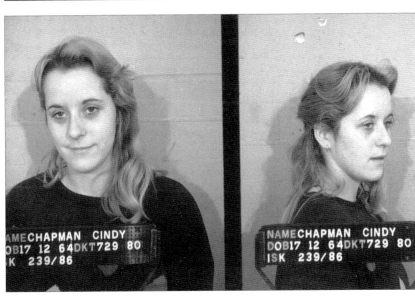

NAME CHAPMAN CINDY
DOB 17 12 64 DKT 729 80
ISK 239/86

NAME CHAPMAN CINDY
DOB 17 12 64 DKT 729 80
ISK 239/86

Me masquerading as an innocent, uniformed cop.

Me masquerading as an ignorant slob – Dean Collie

Top: Indy the cat ... had nine lives, which was eight more than Cindy, the girl who gave her to me.

Bottom: Greg ... we went to school together, he went to jail alone.

Drug raids can be messy. We said we would clean up the town, not drug dealers' hallways after we sledgehammer their doors.

A bandana and a coloured contact lens … just another day at the office, working undercover.

Someone said loud enough for the crook to hear, 'All that rust on the top of the arrow can't be good for you – you don't want that in your blood stream.' Cops laughed in the background.

A few minutes later an ambulance arrived. The two ambulance men looked at the victim, I mean the offender. By now he had lost interest in the debate. He was quietly sobbing. The boss ambulance man said, 'I can try and reduce his pain.'

The offender whimpered, 'Reduce the pain, reduce the pain.'

The ambo guy said, 'But I can't get him off the fence. You will have to call the fire brigade.'

The offender screamed, 'Call the fire brigade, reduce the pain!'

I requested the fire brigade to attend. Darren was talking to a girl or someone on his mobile phone, relaying the story. He just caught the words fire brigade. He said, 'Hey Angus, is he going to catch fire now?' I ignored him. How cruel to make fun of a man in pain.

While we were waiting, I began to explain to everyone how I caught this crook. This annoyed 'the crook' no end. It was quite obvious to all that the only person who caught the crook was himself. But he didn't get the joke. No sense of humour.

The fire brigade arrived and used an angle grinder to cut off the steel fence spike just below his impaled hand. By this time the owner arrived on the scene. He asked me why I put the bloke on the fence. It was a fair question, when you think about it. I told him that the crook did it himself, that he was a burglar I was chasing. The owner said, 'I thought by sharpening the spikes it might put a burglar off, you know, but I didn't think it would actually catch one.'

The owner of the house went inside and came out with a camera. He took a heap of photographs. The crook was not impressed, again.

The owner offered to give me some photos after he had them developed. He was having a great time.

After the fireman cut the fence spike, the owner said, right in front of the crook, 'When you get that out of his hand I want it back 'coz I might catch another one.' We all laughed like drains.

The ambulance man said, 'We will clean it up and get it back to you.' The owner said, 'The rustier the better.'

Throughout the whole incident, no matter now hard the crook tried to make the situation serious, he couldn't. I bumped into him years later in Collingwood. Only then could he laugh about that day. But not as much as I did.

chapter 8

NO WAY OUT

**'We're not the problem, mate,
and you're not the solution'**

IN THE St Kilda days I recall I was looking for a prostitute named Cindy Chapman. Darren and I were in plainclothes and we looked like real shitheads. We were attached to the 'I' District Support Group. I had known Cindy for a couple of years. She was about twenty years old, bottle blonde, with a bubbly personality. She always acted happy in life and was typical of many young street prostitutes before it all caught up with them.

Being a heroin addict, she needed to prostitute herself to make money and, being young and attractive, she made lots of it. The more money she made the more heroin she could buy and use. Having 'track' marks on her arms made her ineligible to work in massage parlours, so the street it was. All she had now was her body.

She was the girlfriend of my old crook mate, Bones. Cindy lived in a shitty old room in a shitty old boarding house. Bones, her boyfriend, and her customers all used the same bed.

Anyway Darren and I decided to go and find Cindy as she might have been with our man Bones. We were after him for an armed robbery or something, or he could have just been a suspect for something. He was always doing something wrong so he was always worth finding. Anyway, we walked to the door of her room. Our guns were concealed in our shoulder holsters. I lifted up my right hand intending to knock politely. For some reason I decided to step back and just kick the door in. After I did, I stepped through the doorway and saw a naked man in the middle of getting his money's worth from Cindy.

This man got a hell of a fright, jumped off Cindy and jumped through a closed glass window. We were on the first floor of the four storey building. Directly below the window was the footpath of The Street.

Cindy and I casually looked at each other. While this man had been getting his money's worth, she had been lying on her back naked on the bed eating an apple.

This sex stuff obviously meant more to him than it did to her. The door being caved in and the customer diving out the window hardly got Cindy's attention.

She gave me a look that indicated that she was disappointed in my behaviour. It made me feel awkward. I rectified the situation by reaching out with my right hand and knocking on the already open broken door three times.

Cindy let her head fall back onto her pillow and smiled. She said, 'Come in.' I said, 'Thanks. Hello Cindy.' I felt it was important to uphold the polite social conventions no matter what the situation, a bit like the missionaries dealing with the natives in darkest Africa.

I walked across the room and looked out the broken window. I said, 'Seen Bones?'

She said, 'He's out scoring. Should be back soon.'

I jerked my head towards the window where the jerk had launched himself into space. 'Do you have that effect on all your clients?' I asked.

She said, 'I wish I had that effect on you. He's just a mug. Must have thought you were going to rob him. He was probably right.' I smiled.

Being naked didn't worry Cindy. She calmly picked up all the mug's clothes, removed $90 for her service fee and $40 for the broken window. She then threw the clothes through the broken glass. The clothes landed on the bloodied naked man who was rolling around on the roadway trying to hold what appeared to be broken ankles.

Next to the bed was a small box with a little tabby kitten in it. Cindy picked up the kitten and said, 'Angus, you want a kitten?'

I said, 'I've just bought a house, I'd love one.'

She said, 'His name is "Indi" – Indiana Jones.'

I said, 'It would need to be.'

That was 1988, twelve years later I still had Indi. At the time of writing he has been run over four times, he has a large scar on his head which causes his right eye to be permanently open, his left front leg was amputated after our next door neighbour found him almost dead in their frontyard after he was hit by a car. He has half a tail after getting it caught in our side fence.

Maybe Indi should have been called Lucky, because he has used up about eight of his lives.

Cindy only had one. She was to die of a heroin overdose in May, 1989.

DARREN called in sick one day. I should have stayed

indoors to do the paperwork, but I wasn't in the mood. In my unmarked car I drove down The Street and slowly went past the St Kilda Cafe and all the shops.

Then I saw Cindy, and accelerated up to her before skidding to a stop. I jumped out of the car, slamming the door, and strode up to her. The Street was packed. Cindy turned in time to see I was coming for her.

She tried to run but I cut her off, pushed her face first onto a rubbish bin and cuffed her.

I said, 'You're under arrest for conspiracy. You're not obliged to say anything, so shut up.' She went ape shit. She used words I'd never heard before. At least not that week.

I put her in the back seat. Meanwhile, several crooks gathered around started to protest about my behavior. They abused me all the way to the car. I sped off.

Cindy abused me, too. I turned and smiled at her and said, 'I thought I might rescue you from those dickheads. You feel like a drink?'

Cindy said, 'You going to pay for my rent, you arsehole? That mug I was with wanted me for an hour.' I threw her the cuff keys. She fiddled around in the back seat trying to undo the cuffs, and eventually managed it. She lit a smoke and climbed into the front seat. No problem in a short skirt.

She looked at me and smiled. 'How's Indi?' she asked.

I said, 'Off the planet, costing me a fortune.' She just smiled again.

We drove to a nice quiet hotel and had a few drinks. We spoke about different cops and different crooks. Most of our conversation was light and happy. At one stage it got a bit heavy.

I spoke to her about her childhood, which she said hadn't been happy.

I spent some time with Cindy. It was a nice break for both of us, for different reasons. A couple of hours later I took Cindy back and dropped her off near The Street. She went back to her world and I went back to mine.

Cindy respected me. Not because I was a copper. It was because I liked her company. She lived off her body. It was all she had left. She used to sort of flirt with me at times. I often thought it was because she was testing me, to see if I would indulge. When I didn't, it gave her a boost to think that someone liked her just because they liked her.

The look we gave each other said it all. No sex required.

ABOUT a month before Cindy died I found her sitting at a table in the St Kilda Cafe. I had gone in there looking for some idiot. Cindy saw me enter and stood up. She walked up and stood in front of me. Her cheeks, upper cheeks, chin, nose, eye lids, lips, neck and arms were covered in disgusting so-called 'love bites'. They were really purple welts. She looked as if she had been violated to the max. The sight of her made me feel sick.

I said, 'Who did that?'

She said, 'A couple of mugs.'

I reached out my right hand and touched her on the upper arm. A sort of feeble comforting gesture. I looked into her eyes and saw nothing but desperation and pain.

She was asking me for help without asking. How could I help her? I was not her pimp. I couldn't protect her. I couldn't get her off the heroin that caused her to prostitute herself in the first place.

I lowered my eyes, looked away. I felt ashamed, but I was not sure why. I thought it was because I couldn't help her. Then I thought it was because I was a male.

I stopped and wondered how cops can protect illegal prostitutes trying to make money to buy heroin. Unfortunately, whenever I think of Cindy I think of her covered in those bites, deliberately violated. When I look at Indi the cat, I often think of her.

A NEW solicitor came to St Kilda. We met in the foyer of our station. I said, 'Constable Angus of St Kilda Police' and he introduced himself as 'Simon Henderson of Henderson, Barker & Associates.

I had arrested a street prostitute named Linda. Someone had seen me pick her up and called Simon to represent her. Linda and I knew she was guilty of the heinous crime of 'possess heroin.' I had been a cop for about three years and that made me an old hand. The new solicitor thought every one of his clients, including Linda, was innocent. The only innocent one was him.

In fact, the only thing Simon thought Linda was guilty of was being a victim of the police. The young lawyer came to The Street thinking the whole game was his. He was so wrong. I'd like to think it was ours, but what I did know for sure was that there were no rules. Simon instantly thought because he was a solicitor and I was a cop, he was superior. To me that was like a stone fish thinking it had it all over a shark.

The day after I met him, I heard a call come over the radio. The call was to attend at his new office. My partner and I attended and Simple Simon met us at the door. Totally embarrassed and obviously out of his depth, he showed me through to the rear of his office. He carefully opened a small toilet door.

There, sitting on the toilet, pants down, legs apart, was Linda. Eyes open, head back, tongue hanging out, saliva down her chin, needle hanging out of her inner right arm. Overdosed on heroin. Obviously guilty and very dead.

I turned to the new smartarse solicitor and said, 'We're not the problem, mate, and you're not the solution.'

Several months later I was interviewing a crook. This crook was desperately trying to give me information so as I would be inclined to allow him bail.

While he was trying to sell his mother, he told me he had committed a large burglary on a liquor store in Prahran. We were talking about how pissed he got when he let drop that he had given his solicitor six bottles of Grange Hermitage in lieu of payment for his legal representation. The crook stated that his solicitor had put them on a shelf in his office.

The perfect part of this story was that his solicitor was Simon Henderson. And they reckon only coppers are always looking for a drink. This was great. I decided to keep this information for a rainy day, as you would.

chapter 9

WRESTLING WITH THE DRUG PROBLEM

'This is better than sex, the hunt'

THE great thing about working plainclothes in St Kilda is that the bosses gave as a bit of a free hand. We weren't burdened down with too many instructions. We were told to get out amongst it. We weren't given specific targets – we just had to go out and get figures.

We targeted whoever we wanted. We targeted the drug dealers. Most coppers went out and got the users and the odd street offender, but it took hard work and time to catch the dealers.

Now, I want to stress that this time was about the best time of my fifteen years in the Police Force. This was the ultimate – we could go out and do what we wanted – when and how we wanted to do it.

I think that heroin traffickers are one of the worst and lowest form of criminal filth. They actively go out and destroy lives and kill people – kill people quickly by deliberately overdosing them and kill people slowly by addicting them. And they just do it for profit, pure greed. I loved to hunt them. It was fun and we were doing good at the same time. Anyway, back to the scene of the crime …

On this particular day we chose to hunt in The Street. We were equipped with our portable radios, guns, cuffs and plainclothes – of course.

I had obtained keys to a large building directly across the road from the St Kilda Cafe. As I have said, the 'Caf' was then the meeting place and the centre of all heroin trafficking in the St Kilda area. It was to drug dealers what the RSL was to old soldiers.

We climbed up the stairs up the back of the building and, using the key I had got from the owners, opened up a door leading to the roof. We crawled flat on our stomachs along the roof to the very edge.

If this job had been in summer we would have been stuffed because there was a line of trees blocking our view, but, being the middle of winter, all the leaves had gone and we could see through the bare branches.

Looking over that edge onto The Street I felt like a kid in a lolly shop. There were so many targets slinking around attempting to hide amongst the 'Joe Citizens'. The crooks tried to blend in with the squareheads, but they always stood out.

I loved to read The Street and see what was happening. It was like looking into a mountain stream and seeing trout hiding in their natural habitat.

I would look at and separate the 'Joe Citizens', the drug users (buyers), the drug traffickers that trafficked purely for the purpose of using themselves (i.e. if they sell four foils of heroin, their dealer gives them one free) and the real target, the greedy blood-sucking parasite known as the non-drug using profiteer.

It was from here we could identify our gallery of targets.

I prided myself on being able to pick them out but there was one that any fool could see. We called him Fat Tony.

He was a very porky pig-faced heroin trafficker and he looked totally out of place. He was in fact an ex-manager and chef of a major restaurant in Prahran who found there was more money in smack than fine dining. He spoke very well and considered himself smarter that everyone.

He came across as being very well-educated and he had a big gold tooth that was always visible due to his incessant sickly smile. Chefs' hours were obviously too long, traffickers' hours were much more reasonable. The profits were much greater and tax free, too.

He had as much class as a fat rat with a gold tooth.

I asked Darren to refresh my memory. 'Didn't we ban him from St Kilda?' I asked.

We had. But there he was, as large as life, walking down Fitzroy Street as if he owned it when, in fact, we did. He turned straight into the fun parlour next door to the St Kilda Cafe. This was an amusement parlour where certain traffickers were known to operate from.

Try as we could in the past we had been unable to charge Fat Tony with trafficking and that pissed us off. Tubs of lard that sell smack should not be able to beat Victoria's Finest.

We'd tried to get prostitutes to purchase smack from him and set him up. We'd tried surveillance of the amusement parlour and using an undercover operative.

I tried every single thing I could think of, including a hidden camera across the road. But there was no way we could get evidence of Tony trafficking.

What he did was traffic from within the amusement parlour so that he could get behind the counter or out the back. He had the heroin hidden in his mouth at times or hidden in the parlour. If we had raided it we would have found a quantity of heroin in the public area under or in one of the many pin-ball machines. We could never prove that it was Fat Tony's.

While we sat on the roof I could feel the beginning of a cunning plan start to form in my cunning head. I loved it when that happened.

The answer was dressed in a big brown leather jacket and jeans (let's call him 'Jacket Man'). He walked nervously up to the entrance of Tony's lair. He saw Tony inside, walked in and about a minute later Jacket Man and Fat Tony appeared at the entrance.

Jacket Man lifted his left arm and pointed to his watch with his right hand. Tony put his arm on Jacket Man's back as though to say, 'trust me, everything will be okay'. They both nodded.

I didn't need a listening device to known what was going on. I interpreted their actions as Tony telling Jacket Man to come back in a few minutes to buy the gear.

Face down, lying on the roof, I smirked at Darren, a look he had seen many times before. 'Don't do it to me,' he said. 'Every one of your brilliant plans turns out to be life threatening, illegal, or both.'

I know that Darren was only joking (I think) and that he actually loved it when the game was afoot. I quickly turned and started to crawl off the roof to the stairwell. Darren followed – a tad reluctantly, I thought.

As we started running down four flights of stairs I heard him yelling at me: 'I hope you've thought this plan all the way through.' He was such a worry-wart. I knew I had to beef up his confidence so I yelled back, 'I've got the first part down pat – we'll just have to ad-lib it from there.'

My long-suffering partner responded: 'Plan's good, ad-lib's bad.'

I was beginning to think he was a pessimist.

We burst out the back of the building so the crooks would never know where we were concealed, hit the back street and kept running. As we did that we passed our unmarked police car.

I puffed to Darren; 'Mate, take the car – he's headed towards Dalgety Street, I'll meet you there – we need him.' I kept running. As far as I could work out, all was going beautifully.

As I arrived in The Street, I spotted Jacket Man turning up a laneway. I stopped running and tried to look casual, walking through the traffic as fast as I could without making too much of a fuss.

I didn't want Jacket Man to see me coming. As I got close to him in the laneway he turned around, realised I was probably a Jack (slang for copper, which is slang for police officer) and started to run. I chased him down onto the roadway as Darren pulled our car up next to us. Jacket Man started screaming, 'I've done nothing!' Why do they always do that?

I informed him that I was going to search him under the Drugs Act for drugs. He said, 'I haven't got any fucking drugs.' He went right off the planet as I began to search his pockets. In his front right hand pocket were five $20 notes. As it happened, $100 was the going price for half a gram of heroin on the streets of St Kilda at the time. Now it is much cheaper, but that is another sad story. He told me his name and other details on request. I looked at Darren and said, 'Can you watch him?' Darren took custody of him while I walked back to our unit to check his current criminal status and see if he was wanted on any outstanding warrants.

I had the $100 with me when I went back to the car. I sat in the car checking out his record, then walked back to Jacket Man and said, 'There are some warrants, you're under arrest.'

I then told Darren to hang on.

I ran back to the cop car and listened to the radio – the crook was too far away to earwig so he couldn't hear. I came back to the crook with a sour face and said, 'This is your lucky day – just go. Darren – armed robbery in progress Carlisle Street, East St Kilda.' I threw the $100 at Leather Man who picked it up and scurried off.

We ran back to the car and Darren did a huge 'burn out' into another side street. We screeched into Acland Street, then Barkly Street, just missing several cars. More method acting at its finest – or so I thought.

I said, 'Okay, that's far enough. Stop.'

Darren looked sideways at me and said, 'But, we're nearly there.'

I quickly confessed, 'Stop, I made it up, drive back to the building we have to see what happens next, quick.'

Darren said, 'What about the armed rob?'

I don't think he was listening. 'Look, I made it up. Just get back, we have to see their next move.'

Darren said, 'Angus, what are you doing?'

I said, 'What we always do, follow the buyer, let the buyer take us to Fat Tony.'

Darren drove to The Street, and parked behind the building

where we first conducting the surveillance. Darren was still shaking his head. I had seen that look before.

He made the point (in a most colourful way) that we were back where we started – at a surveillance post without any evidence.

I was trying to play chess while Darren was still playing draughts.

He said: 'We are just going to sit up this building like every other day and prove nothing'.

I said, 'Wrong.'

We went up the stairs, back on top of the building where we were, crawled along the building, peeped over the side and looked.

I lit a cigarette and blew a confident smoke ring. 'This is better than sex, the hunt,' I confessed. I don't know if Darren agreed with me.

About five minutes later – you guessed it – Jacket Man peeped his head around a laneway into Fitzroy Street to see if it was safe to come out. He was like a moray eel in a leather jacket.

Looking at Jacket Man I willed him out into The Street. 'Come on, Jacket Man, the coast is clear.'

As he carefully walked towards the parlour he took his jacket off as though it was an afterthought. He rolled it up, but had nowhere to hide it. He was no brain surgeon but then, few of them are.

Jacket Man, minus the jacket, was nervously walking up The Street. There was something we could always count on in our hunt for druggies: their desire for heroin was always greater than their sense of self preservation.

As if he was following a piece of string, he made a line

directly to the parlour. As he went out of sight through the doorway, we were on about a forty-five degree angle across the road up on a building. I gave a running commentary to Darren.

Even though I couldn't see, I had a fair idea what was happening. 'Right, he's in. He's taken six steps up to the fat boy.

'Tony walks up and says, "Got the right money? Come over here".

I then spoke in a higher voice for Jacket Man: "Yes Tony, I've robbed the living shit out of everyone. I'm a good little piece of shit that you can suck the guts out of, and I'll do it again tomorrow and the next day".

'Tony says, "That's my boy." They exchange money for gear. Tony pats him on the head and Jacket Man should appear any second.'

You guessed it, just at that moment Jacket Man peeped out the doorway into The Street with Fat Tony right behind him.

The deal was done and Jacket Man took a deep breath as he prepared to run the gauntlet.

I looked at Darren and said: 'That's our cue, let's go!' He rolled his eyes as we moved, keeping low so we couldn't be spotted. 'What's next, Elliott Ness?' I felt a touch of sarcasm creeping into Darren's voice, but perhaps I was being overly sensitive.

As we ran down the stairs he yelled for the thousandth time: 'What are we doing?' I told him our new mission, 'We've got to get the gear, understand, the gear'.

We ran through a few side streets and back out into Fitzroy Street so no-one knew where we came from. As we got close to The Street we stopped running and started to walk. Sure enough, there was our Jacket Man minus the jacket. He was well clear of Fat Tony and he was walking with a pathetic little spring in his step because he had his gear.

I started to stroll across the street. There were two lanes on each side of the tram track that runs up the middle.

I said to Darren: 'Watch this.' I called out to Jacket Man, who was about thirty metres in front of us across the road, 'Hey you.' Jacket Man peeped over his shoulder. 'Yeah you, without the jacket, stop right there! Police.'

I held up my badge to him. Jacket Man exploded into a desperate sprint and I began the chase. Darren followed, but he was clearly starting to lose faith in The Plan. I knew this because he was yelling, 'Are you mad?' I think it was a rhetorical question.

It was obvious we could have walked up behind him and grabbed him by the arm. But Dazza didn't understand that I wanted him to run.

As we ran full bore, he crossed a small road and nearly got run over. More importantly, I nearly got hit as well which was definitely not part of The Plan.

I yelled all the usual lines: 'Stop, Police' and all the rest, and he kept running. I knew he would.

When he realised I was catching him – a copper who smokes should be able to run faster than nine out of ten weedy junkies – he reached into his pocket and tossed a little folded-up piece of paper onto the footpath. I stopped chasing him and picked up the foil of heroin, but as I was bending down I saw Darren whiz past.

I called out: 'Stop, let him go, I've got it.'

Darren had enough of the chase, me, Jacket Man, Fat Tony and The Plan.

Darren was filthy. As I started to walk back toward the parlour my long suffering partner mumbled away behind me, 'Up the stairs, down the stairs, there's an armed robbery, there's no armed robbery, chase this guy, let him go, chase him again, let him go again.'

I think he had low blood sugar. That was what was making him cranky. I couldn't see what else could be the problem.

The way Fat Tony packaged his heroin was quite distinctive. It was a square cut out of a magazine, which contained the gear.

Instead of a foil, (Tony never sold heroin in foils) he sold it in what the drug world calls a 'bindle'. It was cut from a Vogue magazine or similar. Cocaine is normally sold in a bindle, heroin isn't. The heroin bindle was Tony's trademark, basically. He truly was a fat goose.

I said, 'Let's go back and get Tony.'

Darren shook his head (again). 'So we've got enough to arrest Tony now have we? We've seen jack shit, we've got nothing. No buyer, just the 'gear'. We can't prove that Tony sold anyone anything including, that.' He was pointing at the bindle.

I was beginning to think that Darren should get out more often.

I said, 'Watch.'

We walked up and into the parlour. Immediately the place went dead silent. Everyone in there knew who we were.

I reached into my back pocket. Holding up my police badge high in the air I said, 'Relax, it's the police. We are here to protect you from the evils of drugs.'

I walked past several people up to Tony. The tub of lard

was wearing a big golden grin even when I informed him, 'Tony, you are under arrest for trafficking in heroin, you're not obliged to say anything at all, if you do you'll only confuse the situation.'

I turned Tony around and removed my cuffs from the back of my belt. I managed to handcuff one of his wrists but I couldn't get the other cuff on because his other wrist was too fat. This was all much to the amusement of many crooks who were watching. I needed one of the giant leg irons they used to tie up elephants in Thailand to hold him.

By this stage he was wearing an even larger smile. I grabbed his free hand and said, 'All right, just keep your hands together.'

Darren was still just shaking his head in disbelief. Did I tell you he often did that?

Tony said, 'What the fuck are you on about? You've got nothing on me, you know that.'

I walked Tony a few paces toward the door. I stopped him and told Darren to just keep him here for a second. I walked out of the parlour and into a second hand dealer's nearby.

I said, 'G'day, give me that blue light you've got behind the counter there.'

The woman behind the jump said, 'What blue light?' (Why do they always say that?)

I jumped up and over the counter, and she wisely moved back. I reached under the counter and grabbed the ultra-violet blue light.

I said, 'This one.' (Why did I always say that?)

Ultra-violet crayons are commonly used to mark video recorders and such, which helps police identify stolen property. Being a second hand dealer in St Kilda in those days, she used the blue light to see the crayon writing – and then clean it off. She was a scallywag.

I walked back into the parlour, unplugged a large pinball machine and plugged the blue light in. Tony kept on saying in a calm, smartarse voice, 'You've got nothing. My solicitor is going to sue your arse off, you twerp.'

A few of his mates in the parlour seemed to agree, but I wasn't too worried because they didn't look as if they had law degrees. They were saying things like, 'What a load of shit, Tony's done nuffin.'

I faced Tony toward the machine and said in a loud voice, 'Let's test the evidence'

I removed a large fat wallet from large Fat Tony's back pocket. Inside was a large fat amount of cash.

One by one I flipped over each side on the notes, most of the notes were $50s, $20s and $100s. As I started I said, 'Let's look for Exhibit Number One.'

Tony's face changed to a bewildered nervous glare.

As I pulled out each note and held it under the ultra violet blue light I said, 'Gimme number one, come on number one.'

Then 'Bingo, Tony congratulations you're a winner, give the man Exhibit Number One.'

I slapped down a $20 note with the word Exhibit No. 1 written on it. Tony's eye's nearly popped out of his head. I slapped down five $20 notes each with the words Exhibit No.1 written on them. Tony stood there and mumbled 'But, But.' He had lost his big, fat, rat grin.

Darren could not believe it either. The reason we had caught Jacket Man the first time was to mark his money with the invisible ultra violet crayon I had pinched from work. In normal light it is invisible, but under a blue fluorescent light it stood out like a beacon. Tony was in shock and just stood there trying to work it all out.

I said, 'But no, there's more – along with those you get Exhibit number two free.'

I slapped the bindle of heroin down on the pin ball machine. Tony closed his eyes in disbelief. He looked like a cane toad having a power nap.

Tony, Darren and I walked out of the parlour and down the road to our car. I said, 'Tony, I told you not to come back to St Kilda, what goes round comes around – you play in the fast lane long enough, you get run over, mate.'

He shook his head and realised he was gone. He knew that someone set him up and that he'd purchased off an undercover cop. I knew Tony was trying to remember who Jacket Man was. Tony had so many customers he couldn't quite do it.

As we walked down the street Tony started to talk in a low voice sort of from the corner of his mouth. He said things like, 'Listen, just help me and I'll give you anything. Just give me bail, let me go, I'll give you anything.'

I said, 'Anything?'

He said, 'Yeah, what.'

I said, 'I can never make my roast potatoes crispy. I roll them in oil, scratch them with a fork, everything, but I can't get them really crispy.'

He said, 'Please Mr Angus, I'll give you a big dealer.'

All Tony wanted to do was save his arse. Later, he told me that I only had to add a little bit of water to the bottom of the pan just before they finish cooking. He wasn't all bad.

Tony said of Jacket Man, 'So he was a cop, but I thought I knew his sister, or did he just set me up?'

I said, 'Does it matter? You're stuffed either way.' At this time I was on cloud nine – I was absolutely wrapped because I could see in Tony's eyes and I could see in his demeanour that he was a different man, he wasn't the smartarse arrogant fat prick anymore. He was now a big fat nothing.

Tony then started trying to make a deal in the middle of the street. He starts wanting to set up his dealer. He would have sold his mother.

Darren looked at me from behind Tony's back. He was just smiling, still shaking his head, as if he was thinking, 'How the hell did he do that?'

On the way back to the station Tony kept saying, 'Give me bail and I'll set up my main man, he's a big dealer. I just need bail.'

I told him that bail was out of the question. He's just getting locked up and that was that.

In desperation Tony said, 'Listen, my man is coming to my motel room at eight tonight to drop off. I'll set him up, I'll buy off him, just give me bail.'

I refused any such deal, but I found out how to roast spuds properly.

LATER we drove to Tony's motel. We took him up to his room but, by this time Tony was a shattered man. He gave us permission to search it without a warrant which saved a lot of time.

Just to make sure he didn't change his mind I produced a tape recorder from my bag and tape recorded Tony giving us permission. I used a small recorder that takes a normal size audio tape. Tony was trying to be as helpful as possible so we would go easy on him. This sort of tape can be very useful at times. During the search we found the magazine – it was a Cleo or something. You could see where he had cut out lots of square pieces to package the heroin – including the piece that we had.

Tony kept asking, 'Was the guy an undercover cop – was he from interstate, was he from here?'

I just never confirmed nor denied what Tony said. By not confirming or denying the fact that this Jacket Man was an undercover policeman, it convinced Tony that he was absolutely gone, that the weight of evidence against him was massive.

Tony went on to make full admissions to trafficking for the previous three months. By the end of the interview Tony had resigned himself to the fact that he was getting locked up and became his old jovial self.

Darren, Tony and I had a smoke and laughed about all the dickheads we knew around St Kilda. At one stage I asked a young policewoman to sit in the interview room and mind Tony for a minute while we did some of the paperwork.

Tony broke into song. Being an Italian, he appreciated beautiful women. Tony sang an Italian love song in a loud operatic voice with a strong Italian accent. His voice bellowed through the whole station. He was actually very good. The policewoman sat back, enjoying it. I have heard of crims singing in the interview room but not like this.

When the interview was finished it was about 5pm. The court was closed so Tony was remanded in custody by a Bail Justice overnight to front court the next day. Darren and I finished our paperwork and left the station.

As we left I called out, 'See you at Tony's joint later.' Darren said, 'No worries.' I looked at my partner and there was something different about him. Then I realised. He wasn't shaking his head.

Later that night I was making myself at home with my feet up drinking one of Tony's Crown Lagers in front of the TV. There was a knock at the door. It was Darren,

I said, 'Help yourself. There's beer in the fridge, he's even got some spirits and, can you believe it, he's even got an ice maker. I would love a fridge with an ice maker.'

I said, 'Can you believe he had *Scar Face* in his VCR.'

Darren said, 'He cops his right whack in the end.'

The dealer was supposed to turn up at 8pm, but drug dealers are nearly always late. At about 10.15, just when *Scar Face* was about to get really good, and we were a bit pissed, there was a faint knock at the door. Darren jumped up and went into the bathroom. I turned the TV down a bit, I then heard Darren start to run the shower.

I took a deep breath and called out, 'Who is it?'

A deep voice said, 'Alex.' I should have guessed, as every trafficker's name seemed to be Alex.

I carefully opened the door and peeped up and down the hallway. I said, 'Quick, come in.'

Alex was Romanian or something. He had the gold chains happening, black leather jacket and the usual gear on. I still don't know why drug dealers always seem to dress like drug dealers. Maybe there was a shop where they all bought their clothes. It could be called: 'Big Bucks No Taste.'

Alex quietly came in. I held out my hand and said, 'I'm Wayne, Tony's brother-in-law. Well, ex-brother-in-law. Well, she's not Tony's real sister, she's a …'

Alex cut me off. He wasn't interested in my ramblings.

'Where's Tony,' he asked suspiciously.

I said, 'In the shower.'

We could see steam coming from beneath the bathroom door.

I said, 'I'll get Tony, but he's really pissed off that you're late.'

Alex said, 'Well, fuck him.'

I said, 'Hang on a sec.'

I was just about to open the bathroom door when Tony's voice burst into the air. I opened the door and through the steam I could just see Darren. We had Tony's stereo system on his toilet and we had taped Tony singing to the police-woman at the station.

I made out I was talking to Tony in the shower.

I said, 'But I don't want to get involved – but, but, okay, Christ.'

I left the bathroom and closed the door. The tape started again and Tony's voice sang out again, 'Mi, O, Mi, AHHHH, COME HOME TO MEEEEEEEE.' That sort of thing. It loses something in the translation.

'Tony told me where the money is and he wants me to do the business.

Alex hesitated, and said, 'I get it.' I don't think he did.

Alex left and returned seconds later. We sat on the couch and Alex put three ounces of rock heroin on the table. I reached over and picked up a large vase in the middle of the table and turned it upside down. Nothing came out so I shook it again. My police badge fell onto the table. I picked it up and showed him. And said: 'You're under arrest.'

Alex reached over and took the badge from me and looked at it closely. He was the studious type. I pointed out and said, 'See that writing, it says TENEZ LE DROIT. That means

UPHOLD THE RIGHT.' I touched my chest with both hands and said, 'That's what I do.'

Alex was convinced. He jumped up, pushing me away. I had a huge struggle with him. Not a stand-up punching match, just an all out full-on, old-fashioned Greco-Rumanian wrestle.

At this point Darren should have burst out of the bathroom to assist because what is the point of having a partner if he is not there to help gang up on the crims?

But there was no Darren. He was still sitting on the edge of the bath in the steam-filled bathroom with Tony's voice blaring away full blast.

It was like an opera in a Turkish bath. Darren couldn't hear me calling for help. After several minutes I managed to handcuff Alex's left ankle to his right wrist. I was stuffed and he wasn't much better.

Darren then peeped out of the bathroom. I saw his face and said, 'Yeah mate, it's safe to come out now.'

He said, 'You've got the bad guy.' On the table was a large amount of heroin. We were proud of ourselves and we had every reason to be.

As usual, we didn't have handcuff keys so we had great difficulty in getting Alex down the stairs of the motel and into the cop car, and going into the station was fun as well. He looked like a giant Rumanian Pretzel.

We worked through the night interviewing and charging Alex.

When we fronted court that morning we both looked like death. The crooks looked better than we did. It had been a big twenty-four hours.

Tony's case was up first and I applied to have him

remanded in custody. It was very funny because at court when I was in the witness box giving evidence, Tony's Legal Aid barrister asked me the identity of the mysterious Jacket Man.

I told the Court that his name was Mark Bowers. I went on to say that I had in fact checked him after I'd seen him approach Tony, and that I thought he was going to return a few minutes later and buy heroin from the fat man.

I told the court how I marked the buyer's money without him knowing, and then gave the money back to him. Tony's face started to change as he woke to what had really happened – he started to realise that the whole thing was a scam.

I then went on to say that from the roof, I observed Bowers re-attend at the parlour and walk in towards Tony. I told the court that when he came his demeanour had changed and he had a spring in his step.

I told the court the whole story of how we caught Fat Tony and how he made admissions of trafficking for the past three months.

Tony just shook his head (he must have caught the habit from Darren) as he realised the whole thing was a smoke and mirrors job and that he'd put himself in.

The penny dropped that he'd convinced himself he was stuffed when in fact he wasn't, and if he hadn't made any admissions he would have walked away and not been charged. With all the evidence we had gathered, when you put the whole thing with his admissions, he was absolutely gone. The magistrate found it amusing. So did I.

Tony's barrister, the poor dear, tried his best by accusing me of tricking Tony and lying to him. I looked at the magistrate with a George Washington look and said: 'I certainly did not lie. When he asked me several times who Jacket Man was, I just refused to confirm or deny the fact that he was, or was not, an undercover operative.'

I informed the court that I had some concerns about Mark Bowers (Jacket Man) looking like an informer and setting up Tony. I told the court I wanted to make it quite clear that, at that time Mark Bowers had no idea that I had marked the money and he had no idea I would return that paper bindle full of heroin back to Tony. Of course, on top of it all, the cream was finding the magazine that matched this square piece of paper.

You could also see other squares had been cut out of the magazine. They often said that solving crime was like putting together a jigsaw. This time they were right.

The magistrate remanded Tony in custody. As Tony was leaving the dock he stopped as Alex was led out of a door in front of him into the dock. Tony looked terrified as he turned and looked at me. I gave him a wry smile and lifted my eye brows as if to say, 'Life's a shit sandwich.'

I think he agreed with me.

ONE day Darren and I were working plainclothes when I received information from an old crow about an old guy whose name was Eddie Tout, who was known around The Street as 'the Trout'.

He was about seventy-three years old and still sold heroin from the St Kilda Cafe. What he did was keep his heroin in those stainless steel straw dispensers that sat in the middle of the counter within the cafe. It was a pokey little cafe with six tables and chairs and the the main counter.

Anyway, he would sit on a stool in the middle of the

counter. He'd sit there with heroin concealed inside this stainless steel straw container. He paid the owner $20 an hour to sit on the stool in the cafe, waiting for junkie customers.

So we looked for him that day, but every time we went there he was missing, so we decided at the end of the shift to stay back and do surveillance.

We finished work, went and bought a six-pack of Fosters and sat directly over the road from the cafe on a window sill in the frontyard of a big old house.

We sat on the window sill with our feet dangling about a foot off the ground drinking cans and having a smoke, determined to catch this old bloke as the pinch seemed pretty simple. In front of us was about five metres of lawn then a small front fence. So there we sat.

Anyway, it started to get a bit dark and then, of course, we ran out of cans and any off-duty surveillance was out of the question without lubrication, so we had to go to the Prince of Wales hotel for another six-pack. We had to get our priorities right.

When we returned two females kept standing in front of us while we were trying to look at the cafe. We kept looking around them, trying to look across the road, but we both wished they'd piss off out of our way.

Then, all of a sudden, a great big, young bloke of around eighteen who we'd never seen before, walked up and started talking to them. Then they were all right in our way. So we kept leaning around trying to see. If he hadn't been so big we would have told him to piss off.

So there we were – contorting ourselves, bending over, looking around them wishing they'd piss off, when the big one said, 'Right, what do you want?'

I nudged Darren. He looked at me and said quietly, 'You're kidding?'

One of them said, 'We just want one – just a half.'

He said, 'Sweet – no problem.' Anyway, they either didn't see us sitting on the window sill or they didn't give a shit about us.

He started to reach down inside his jocks when one of the females said, 'Hey listen, can you spot us $10, we've only got $80' (because a half of heroin was $90).

The big, fat, young bloke turned around and said, 'Get fucked – pay the price or fuck off' or words to that effect. She started, 'Please, please, we're $10 short, we'll give you an extra $10 next time.'

He's saying, 'Yeah, yeah, sure. You're full of shit.' They start arguing and bargaining and as two girls tried to get a discount – it was just ridiculous. It was all there right in front of us.

So we're looking at each other. We think, 'Oh well, what the hell'. We skolled what was left of our cans. By this time the bloke had finally agreed. He was not happy about it. The girls started to count out the money into his hand. He started to get the heroin from the inside of his jocks.

I whispered words similar to, 'The girls are on my side – I'll take them.'

Darren said, a bit sarcastically, 'Oh, leave me the fat bloke?'

I whispered, 'I'm a lover not a fighter,' or words to that effect and Darren called me a bastard, or words to that effect. At least he didn't shake his head this time.

Darren had to take the big bloke. I've just jumped out, held my badge at the two girls 'Get on the ground, don't move! Police.' Darren, of course, drew his gun on the big fat bloke

Sometimes, crooks brought us to our knees.

Toys for bad boys ... a Luger with a silencer, a machine pistol, a machine gun and a couple of glorified water pistols.

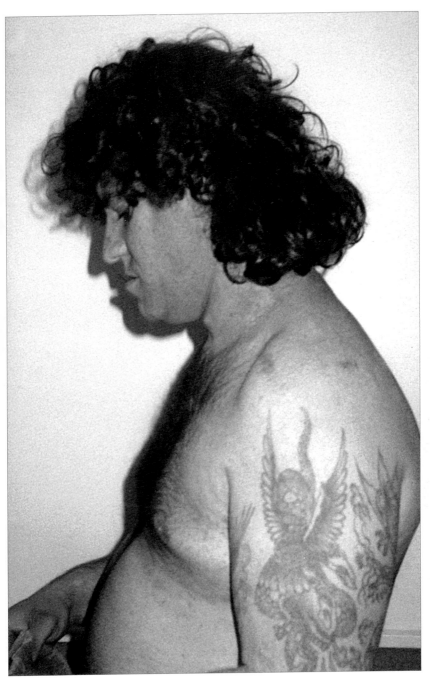

The Bear … a tough crook who lost his gold chain, but not his bottle.

Have you busted a Ford lately? Me with a drug dealer's pride and joy.

Taking it lying down … an unhappy dealer shows where he keeps his gear.

Me, serious for once, the day I rescued a child from a deranged man.

Setting a white pointer to catch a fish finger … our undercover agent, Marielle Porter, in the celebrated flasher case.

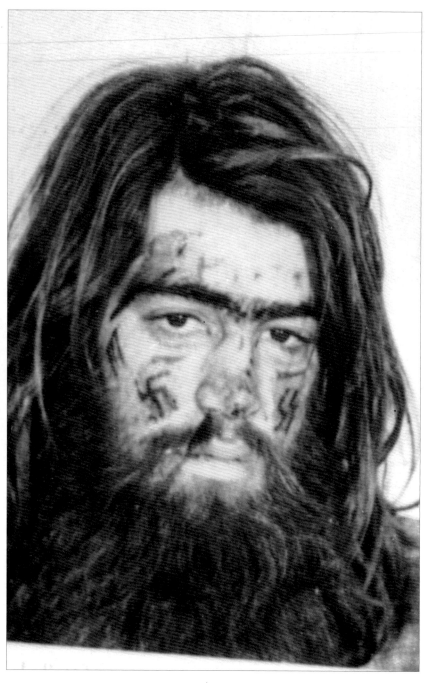

Werewolf? Charles Manson? Undercover cop? No, just another loser.

and told him to get on the ground. But the fat bloke was young and stupid and decided to argue the toss.

I got the girls down on the ground without much problem.

I stepped around behind the big bloke to stop him getting away. Darren realised that the gun wasn't having the desired effect and reluctantly started to put it back in its holster, realising it was going to be a fight. It was time for Plan B.

I knelt down on all fours behind the fat bloke, Darren shirt fronted him with his shoulder and tried to push him backwards so I would trip him over, but the fat bloke didn't budge and Darren bounced off him onto the ground. The fat bloke just stood there and pushed me out the way with his foot and started to walk off. So much for Plan B.

We both jumped up onto the fat bloke and I screamed at the two girls, 'Stay on the ground, you're under arrest.' At first the girls obeyed and lay there face down. The fat bloke just kept pushing and pulling us off him and dropping us over the small brick fence.

I recall being very careful not to punch this bloke. The first reason was that it would have no effect on him, anyway. The second reason was that I didn't want him to punch me back. So a wrestle it was.

After a minute or so the two girls ignored our screams not to move, stood up, brushed themselves off and quickly walked to freedom. Darren and I were by no means winning the wrestle. In fact, the fat bloke started to walk off down the street dragging us with him. It was like two flyweights attacking a Sumo.

People came over and watched. We should have sold tickets.

In the middle of the wrestle Darren screamed, 'Cuff him, cuff the bastard.'

I screamed back, 'I don't think he's at the cuffing stage just yet, you idiot.'

Darren and I were exhausted.

Then I started trying to pull his pants down. The fat bloke thought he was being attacked by a crazed homosexual copper. I finally got them over his belly down to his ankles, which stopped him walking and tripped him over. Once he was on the ground it was a bit easier to wrestle him.

I said, 'Get your cuffs out.'

Darren said, 'I haven't got cuffs, you're supposed to have the cuffs, I had the radio.'

I said, 'Use the radio.'

Darren said, 'I forgot it.'

I yelled, 'You don't bring the cuffs because you've got the radio, but you haven't got the radio!'

Darren and I kept arguing while we fought this bloke.

After about five minutes I got sick of it. The big fat guy was face down. I pulled out my gun and pushed it hard into his right ear. I was puffing so much I could hardly breathe. I said, 'NOW, I'm ready to shoot you. Give me two big blinks if you believe me.' Fat guts gave me two big blinks. I was very happy.

The next moment about five police cars with their lights and sirens going pulled up. All the coppers who turned up laughed at the sight before them.

Meanwhile a large crowd of people had built up around us.

I said to Darren, 'Have you got the gear – the foil?'

Darren said, 'No, I thought you were picking it up.' We argued again about who was going to pick up he foil.

We crawled around in the tan bark and found one of the foils. We took fat guts back and charged him with trafficking heroin.

We'd gone hunting a wily old trout and landed the great white whale.

THE following day we again worked, but still couldn't find the Trout. After the shift we were still determined to crack the case (and a few cans). We headed back to the window sill. We were on our first can when this old grey-haired bloke wearing a suit walked into the cafe.

We gave him a couple of minutes to get set up, followed him in and there he is sitting there at the counter with a straw dispenser right in front of him. We sat either side of him, and went into the routine.

'G'day mate – how's it going? We're plainclothes cops,' I said, and we showed him our badges.

I looked at the straw dispenser. 'What are we going to find in this, mate?' I asked. He looked at me and said, 'What do you reckon?'

I tipped it upside down. About a dozen foils of heroin were stuck to the bottom of the straw dispenser with blue tack. He said, 'Never seen them before in my life.' For some reason we didn't believe him.

Because the straw dispenser was stainless steel you could see fresh fingerprints on it. I said, 'Well, whose fingerprints are they, do you reckon?' He just looked at me in silence.

I said, 'You're under arrest for trafficking in heroin.'

As we walked him out and down the street. He said, 'So I'm fucked, aren't I?' and I said, 'Yeah Digger, you are'.

We had hooked the Trout.

He gave me the impression he would have been a real good

crook in his day. Anyway, we got back to the station and he was being quite friendly and talkative. He explained how he'd been a crook most of his life. He spoke of being in the war and about his past.

I got him a hot cup of coffee. He took two sugars.

'Do you know this cuppa is the first thing I have ever taken from a copper in me life? Besides a beating, that is,' he said.

He then let out a long sigh and said, 'I'm too old this crap.'

A short time later I interviewed him about trafficking heroin. He made full and frank admissions to trafficking for the past week out of the St Kilda Cafe. But he did it without lagging anyone else.

At the end of the interview I sat in front of him and had a chat. I said, 'What's your caper? Records state that you only ever say 'No Comment' when interviewed. Should we feel privileged or what?'

He said, 'I'm too old for this shit. I've been interviewed by some of the best in my day. I remember that bastard Detective Sergeant (name deleted) from Coburg CIB interviewed me about a safe break. I told him nothin', so he threw me out the interview room window head first and charged me with escape! I still told him nothin'.' The Trout started to cry.

Reading his history was interesting. His antecedents said that every cop who ever met him said he was unco-operative, would never say anything or admit to anything.

He had been an armed robber in his younger years, then a safe breaker. He had been in the war and his wife had died. He had two priors for trafficking heroin which resulted in jail terms.

He was now seventy-three. He was proud of his age and

told everybody. I found it strange that he was making full admissions at the time.

Maybe I was the friendliest copper he had ever run into over all those years. Or maybe he was just getting old and sentimental and I got lucky.

When we finished the paperwork we bailed him, because of his age and the fact we had proved where he lived and his identity. He left the station. Darren and I left for home a bit later. The next morning we came to work and a policewoman said to me, 'Oh, did you hear what happened?'

No, we hadn't. The policewoman said, 'That drug trafficker you charged last night, Eddie Tout. Did you hear?'

I said, 'No, what?'

She said, 'You let him go a 19.30 and he hanged himself at 19.45.'

Fifteen minutes after we let him go he walked back to his car, drove home and hanged himself in a tree at the front of his house. One of the neighbours found him.

Even to this day I think he was trying to make some sort of a little statement by doing it so openly. I realised why he was so co-operative and why he made full admissions for the first time in his life. He had reached the end.

I was disappointed that I hadn't picked it up in the interview. I'd known something was wrong and I found it strange he was making admissions, but I didn't put it all together.

To be honest, you try not to care if they just go and shoot themselves, deliberately overdose, hang themselves or whatever, and often you don't. But this old guy – I often remember him.

Some time later I read his autopsy report. It turned out he had forty-seven puncture marks in his thighs. There was only one explanation for that, and I would never have picked it. He regularly injected heroin. He was a junkie.

The more experience I had as a copper, the more I realised I didn't know.

I WAS driving down Grey Street with my mate Darren when we saw a well known prostitute called 'Katrina.' She saw us approaching and started to walk away, but I called her over.

Katrina was a quite attractive. Tall, slim, twenty three years old, with long legs in high heels. She walked straight up to the passenger side window, which was open.

She lifted her tight little top and thrust her large breasts into Darren's face and said, 'Please don't book me, please.'

As a few members of the public could see what she was doing it was quite embarrassing, being a cop with naked tits hanging in your window.

I smiled and said, 'Katrina, put them away, you could poke someone's eyes out with them. Any new dealers around that you want to talk about?'

She pulled her top down and said, 'There's an old "Straight Head", got heaps of gear. He turned up last week. Called Stan. About seventy, grey hair, well dressed. You'll find him first table on the left at Joe's Pizza.' I thanked her and we left.

We sat off Stan and watched him deal for about half an hour. One of the people he sold heroin to was a shit head named Blackie.

I walked up to Stan and said I was a mate of Blackie's. Stan sold heroin to me. When Darren and I arrested him he said, 'Oh, I guess I'm in a spot of bother, I'm terribly sorry.' We took him back to our office. Stan was strange. He was very well-spoken and obviously didn't belong in Fitzroy Street. He had never been in trouble in his life. He was a mathematician or scientist who had been a university lecturer. He presented as most professional. Get this, the reason he was selling heroin was that he reckoned he had found the answer to winning at roulette.

He had found the secret formula of how to place his bets to win every time. It's just that he had been losing a lot, but he would fix that if he could just bet again. His pockets were full of notes and formulas. He sold heroin to make money to prove this formula.

He was an addict, but not a smack-head – he was a gambling addict.

He had 'discovered' he could sell heroin and make a lot of money. Darren and I were the first cops to meet him. I asked him where he got his heroin from and he told us he got it from a high level Rumanian drug dealer by the name of Alex. Another Alex – a smart Alex.

This Alex was about thirty two, with the mandatory moustache, leather jacket and dark sunglasses. He drove a late model flashy car, delivered only on the outskirts of St Kilda, would never go near The Street and he delivered nothing short of an ounce of pure, which was about twelve grand at the time.

We decided to get Alex.

A new policewoman named Jane had just arrived at St Kilda. She'd been at our station for about two days. She was a young, slightly plump, attractive girl who was nineteen and looked fifteen.

She was short with a very pretty young face. I saw the Sergeant, told him that we had this guy who was buying ounces at a time who was willing to set up a dealer. I needed an undercover girlfriend and Jane was perfect.

I convinced him that we could teach her and that she could do it. The Sergeant agreed we could have her for a couple of days. He also asked us to be careful with her. Us careful? Of course. We then went and saw young Jane, sat her down and told her we would like her to assist us and be my girlfriend undercover.

She thought it sounded great. She also said she knew nothing about drugs. I said, 'Well, we'll go out for a drink and I'll teach you all you need to know'.

We gave her a crash course on drug dealing, how it's bought, the slang terms, how it's cut up, etc. I explained the following levels of drug users and dealers:

1) The heroin user buys 'caps', also known as 'foils'. These contain anything from .15 of a gram to .5 of a gram of heroin depending on the purity.

2) The next level is the heroin trafficker who gets about five foils from a dealer. If he sells four he can keep one for nothing. He then gives the money he got for the four foils and gets given another five. This keeps repeating. This is the common 'street dealer' or 'user dealer'.

3) Then there is the dealer who may supply several other street dealers. He too is often a drug user himself, but can also be making a tidy profit, which is mostly spent on using larger amounts of heroin, gambling and cars.

4) The high level drug trafficker that deals for pure greed makes large amounts of money. He can afford to purchase large amounts of heroin very cheaply, and often dilutes it to maximise his profits.

5) Last of all, you have the importer. The importer can

purchase a pound of pure rock heroin in Thailand for next to nothing. Once in Australia it can be sold for about $105,000 wholesale.

Profits are huge, but you risk the death penalty bringing it out of Thailand. Your profits can be even larger if you can sell the heroin yourself down the trafficking pecking order because the closer you can sell to street level the bigger the profit, because you cut out the other levels.

I explained all this over drinks. We then formulated a plan. The plan was for Jane and me to act as heroin purchasers from Perth. We came from Perth because the heroin is a lot cheaper in Melbourne. This time we would want just one ounce of pure rock, but next time we came over we would want a lot more.

The bait, as always, was greed.

We set up in a motel room. We would stay only for one day and then, our story went, we would be flying back to Perth. That way they couldn't stuff us around for long. Professor Stan was to organise the meeting and the first introduction would be in the motel room.

The following day, Darren, myself and Jane were given permission to work on this one job full time. We then went down to the local motel and spoke to the manager who we knew and trusted. We got a room for nothing.

We then set up the room. We bought heaps of shit in there to make it look as if we had just arrived. Jane got some stuff in from her home and it looked as if a couple had just unpacked.

Stan came over and we told told him all he needed to know. He then rang Alex from our motel room and arranged for him to come over in an hour just to organise the deal. Alex was a pretty switched-on drug dealer. He liked the idea of meeting with Jane, but refused to meet the boyfriend. At the end of the call I asked Stan why he didn't want to meet me. Stan finally admitted that he had told Alex that I was a jail escapee from Perth and was 'hot to trot'. Alex (they didn't call him Smart Alex for nothing) thought he might get robbed.

The last thing we needed was an elderly mathematician turned roulette nut turned scag seller trying to make things up as he went along. I laid the down the law to Stan, telling him not to say a word unless he was told.

Stan's story made things quite difficult as Jane had to do it alone and we needed to cover her closely.

As a drug dealer the most dangerous thing that can happen is getting robbed and undercover operatives are not exempt. All precautions must be taken to cover this possibility. Rip-offs are part of the scene.

Alex said he'd come about an hour after Stan gave him the name of the motel and room number. We then started briefing Jane, getting ready for the meeting. Here was a kid just out of the academy who was now going undercover with a partner.

Within about ten minutes there's a knock at the door – Alex was the only dealer in the history of the world to be early. I then looked at Jane and mouthed the words, 'Who is it?' and Jane called out 'Who is it?' on cue.

There was this deep Rumanian voice that said, 'It's Alex – open the door'. I jumped into the shower recess and Darren jumped into the toilet. Old Stan was still there, of course.

So the door was opened and in he came for the meeting.

He appeared to like Jane very much as she certainly didn't even look old enough to be a policewoman. He trusted Stan because he was a good dealer and had dealt with Alex for quite some time. Alex told Jane how they met at the casino playing roulette.

Now the deal was that Jane and I were from Perth, that heroin was more expensive in the West, that Stan had spent a lot of time in Perth previously and Jane's boyfriend was like a grandson to him.

It sounded like crap, but Alex seemed to cop it. Everything was going fine, then Alex asked to see Jane's air tickets. Fortunately I had gone to Tullamarine and got the woman at the counter to make me up a couple of bodgie tickets that showed us flying in a couple of days earlier.

This fitted our story perfectly so Alex was assured when he saw the tickets. Jane arranged to buy one ounce of heroin for $12,000 at St Kilda Pier, at the cafe at the end of the pier, the following night. The deal was set for 7pm.

While I was hiding in the shower I was wearing a grey jacket that I always wore and it had a sort of belt thing at the bottom of it and two steel rings that hang down at the back. I know a lot about drug dealers, but not a lot about fashion.

Anyway, while I was in the shower recess I moved and tapped the two rings against the tiles of the shower and for a moment I thought the experienced member was going to blow the operation while the rookie was starring. Luckily, Alex didn't seem to hear anything.

We were happy for Jane to be up front because she was perfect. She had a bubbly, lively personality and sold the whole thing beautifully.

Alex left, we came out and told Jane she'd done a great job. Jane just about collapsed, fell back on the bed in this motel room and said, 'That was sensational'. She loved the experience. She'd never dreamed she was suddenly going to arrive from the academy and buy $12,000 worth of heroin undercover.

Anyway, the next day we organised buy/bust teams. We got plainclothes, the CIB, the dog squad, everybody we could think of to bust Alex.

We had search and rescue on stand-by. We had cops everywhere to try to follow him and pick him up. Our plan was to find out where Alex was getting his heroin and to arrest his supplier. We didn't just want Alex, we wanted his supplier so we could go up the ladder.

I briefed everyone that Alex might be early so we were set up and were ready by 5.30pm. Time passed, and by 7.30pm I could not hold on to my little police army any longer. The bosses would not authorise any more overtime.

It was a 'no show' on Alex's behalf. Nothing. We didn't have his phone number, only a pager number. I paged him several times, but still nothing.

Eventually, to my embarrassment, I had to tell everybody the deal was not going ahead, and they could all leave. We left the pier. It was a disaster. Everybody was laughing at us. Somehow, I was getting used to it.

Stan couldn't get on to Alex either. I was about to take Jane home when she told me she left her keys back at the motel and I had to go back there anyway to pick up our gear.

I told Jane that we had to be quick to make sure we didn't bump into Alex. You only want to deal with a dealer on your terms. The problem was that Alex might want to go ahead with the deal and all our covering cops had gone home for fish fingers in front of the TV – *Blue Heelers* was on, I think.

We threw our gear into bags and left the motel room, but as

we approached reception, you guessed it, Alex arrived. Jane said, 'You're too late, Alex.'

I tried to get on the front foot, 'So this is the bloke that stuffed us around.'

Alex said, 'I spoke with Stan, he said you were upset. I'm sorry, we can still do it. Somebody stole my car in Dandenong, I was stuck.'

I said, 'You left me on the end of a pier with twelve grand. I'm not interested in you, you're fucking unreliable, you're full of shit. You only understand day time and night time. I need to know when it's happening because I've got business to do. You're late – no business. Simple. I've got a reputation, we have to get it somewhere else.'

Alex said, 'But I've got it now. I will pay for your airfare – please.'

I said, 'Just get out of my face, I've organised it with someone else, my word is my word; you're a fuck up.'

He pleaded so much it was obvious that he had committed himself and had to sell the gear. He may have got it on credit or something, because he was desperate.

I called out to the receptionist: 'Can we have the same room for another night?'

She didn't look up. 'Yes, certainly.'

I said to Alex, '10 am tomorrow, here, one 'Aussie' (slang for an ounce) Take $900 off for airfare and this motel, I'll give you $11,100. Your boss delivers it – if I see you anywhere near here the deal's off, do you understand? If all goes well this time that means I can trust you again, you do it next time. Tell your boss if I'm happy with this one, I want six ounces of rock every Friday.'

He said, 'Yes, that's okay, but I can do it?'

I said, 'You heard me – yes or no?'

Now Alex was on the back foot, 'That will be fine. Ten tomorrow. Trust me.'

We returned back to our room and Alex left. Jane said, 'Well, you might have done that before. I don't think this was your first time.'

I said, 'Once or twice. These cockheads have to show a bit more professionalism. Some of these idiots give drug dealers a bad name. The bottom line is "Money talks, bullshit walks".'

We dropped all our gear on the bed, sat down and cracked a couple of cans of bourbon and coke. I telephoned Darren and told him the good news. He muttered something about trying to convince everyone it would happen again tomorrow. I couldn't see him, but I bet he was shaking his head.

The next morning we set up surveillance all around the motel. We had an arrest crew set up in the motel room next door. We waited until 10am came and then waited some more. You don't have to be told – no show.

Eventually an unknown man walked past our door. Everyone thought he was not our man, but he turned and knocked on our door. I opened it and he came right in. He was a long-haired smartarse, wearing sunglasses indoors, a leather jacket, all the usual dealer shit. He said, 'Call me Peter.'

I said, 'You can call me Paul.'

He smiled and said, 'I'll call you Lenny'. I let him think he knew more than I did.

I pulled out the cash and dropped it on the table. Peter said, 'I'll come back.'

Peter left to get the 'gear'. Surveillance had reported a late model Ford circling the motel. Peter met the driver out the front and the driver handed him a small package. Peter returned to the room.

And as soon as he shut the door he, Jane and I were arrested by a bunch of screaming, lunatic coppers. Sometimes I think we would be safer being raided by crooks. Another unit arrested the bloke in the car.

Cops always over-do it. There is always too many of them and they always get too excited. For some reason they love hurting undercover cops in the arrest.

Maybe they didn't like me or maybe they were just bored. They probably think there's method in their madness, in that they try to sell the idea they're arresting real crooks all round, and biff the undercovers to make it look good. But, having been on the receiving end of such fraternal enthusiasm more than most, I reckon it's more a case of too much madness in their method acting.

Anyway, what's a few bruises between friends when it all works a treat? It was a great pinch. The heroin turned out to be about ninety-one percent pure, the highest seen at the Victorian Science Laboratory at that time.

Back at the station Peter became most upset when I walked into the interview room being led by Darren. I had my head down, hands behind my back in the handcuff position. Peter said, 'Anything is his. I know nothing, if you have drugs or something it is his. I am innocent, I have a family, I do nothing, I swear on my mother's grave he do it, not me.' Peter was crying. I nearly believed him. Nearly.

I lifted my head, moved my hand in front of me and lit a smoke. Darren and I sat down in front of him. I smiled and blew smoke into his face. I said, 'I thought I could trust you. If we can't trust each other how can we ever do business?'

Peter's face dissolved as his life flashed before him. He closed his eyes as he realised he was about to spend several years in jail. Darren, Jane and I had a laugh. It was a very good pinch. We halted the interview to go and search Peter's house. It was a huge joint. He had money to burn and, of course, that's what he did. You should have seen the shit he wasted it on. Such as the huge, purple, velvet-covered stereo bedhead. To ethnic drug dealers these bed-heads were mandatory. He should have got five years for bad taste.

We found a small quantity of heroin and some packaging, but nothing of any great importance.

After the interview we conveyed Peter over to the local court. Word had spread, via his upset wife no doubt, and the court was packed with Peter's cousins, uncles and brothers. They all looked like younger and older versions of Peter.

We were all smiling at Peter's misfortune. Until Peter called out to one of his relatives in Rumanian or similar. I could not understand a word – except the name Alex.

I had decided not to charge Alex with conspiracy or attempting to traffic heroin because I wanted to protect Stan. If I charged Alex it meant Stan was the informer. If I let Alex go then no-one would be positive.

During the remand hearing at court I saw several relatives leave the court. I had to stay.

About half an hour later Peter was remanded into custody. We left the court. I drove over to Stan's home and spoke with him. He told me he had spoken to Alex about thirty minutes before and that Alex had no idea Peter had been arrested.

Darren, Jane and I drove to Alex's house and found him at home. He was lying dead in his doorway. He had been badly beaten and a syringe was sticking out of him. I checked him, returned back to the car and called it in to VKC. I requested homicide attend.

All three of us imagined Alex trying to tell Peter's criminal associates that he didn't set Peter up. Nothing we could have said to Peter after his arrest would have helped Alex. I signed Alex's death warrant the second I kicked him out of the drug deal.

I'm not sure if I did it without realising the consequences or I just didn't care. I did know the sight of Alex's body wiped the smile off my face. It brought home the fact that all this is not a game. The death of a drug dealer is a death, is a death, is a death. We all felt we'd been touched by it.

I knew I wasn't responsible, but I wasn't innocent either. Welcome to The Street, Jane.

A TOP mate of mine was Chooka. I worked with him at St Kilda. He was newly married to a police woman named Karen, who also worked at St Kilda. She was one of the boys – and one of these girls that could melt you with a smile. We used to go fishing – well, it was actually a big card playing weekend at Chooka's parents' holiday house at Inverloch.

No girls, just us blokes. We would get pissed for three days and come home. Anyway, we got back from one of our annual trips to find trouble.

When Chooka got home, his newly-wedded wife Karen asked him to leave for good. He was devastated. Chooka left home and stayed with his sister in her flat. Karen said she was totally sick of all his bullshit. Chooka worshipped the ground she walked on. Everyone knew she was a great catch, especially for Chooka, but he was a real lad, one of 'the boys'.

Anyway, Karen was working at our plainclothes office. She was slim and attractive, very serious and frighteningly intelligent.

She didn't just think she was never wrong, she was never wrong, and could turn you into stone with a look. Really tough, smart women always scare the living shit out of blokes, including me.

About three days later Chooka came to work pissed. It was 8am. I fronted him to find what was wrong.

I told the sergeant I was taking him home to look after him. So we went straight to the nearest pub instead, to sort it out (as you would).

I then discovered the real problem. Chooka told me that he had gone home the night before to pick up a few things. He found that Karen was living with another policewoman from St Kilda. He found that the spare bedroom was not set up. He had said to Karen: 'Is she staying in our bed, our wedding bed just like you and me?'

Karen had told him, 'Yep, she's what I want, she gives me what I need.'

Well, that nearly killed him. He still loved her. To have her leave him for a woman was devastating, not to mention highly embarrassing.

He decided to fix the problem by getting pissed every day forever. It was a Monday when I discovered this gem. It was always going to be a big day, as it was Filthy's last day in The Job.

Filthy (his real name was Phil) had been a copper for thirty-one years. He was one of the first cops to seriously work undercover. Phil had made sergeant fifteen years before and was happy to stay at that rank.

He was an Aussie, but he looked more like an old Italian fisherman than a cop. He was a lovely bloke, but could never just have a couple of drinks and go home. Once he started that was it, he drank till he dropped.

It didn't take long for Filthy to hear that Chooka and I were down the pub already. Filthy's last day drinkathon was not due to start until 5pm but here we were, getting into it at about 9am. (I got the publican to open the bar early for us.)

I was drinking Coke, and every now and then I would have a light beer. I had decided to be sensible – at least until 5 or 6pm.

Anyway, about 6pm six of us decided to change pubs and head to the Prince of Wales in Fitzroy Street. So six very scruffy undercover cops poured themselves into an old 'Rent-a-Bomb' Ford Cortina.

Filthy and Chooka were 'maggotted'. We were all squashed, sitting on each other's laps. As the driver, I was constantly telling everyone to just calm down and not be silly.

As we were driving along everyone in the back seat decided that Filthy looked as if he was about to vomit. To be on the safe side they took the risk of moving Chooka – who could also vomit at any moment – out of the way so they could shove Filthy over to the rear seat driver's side window. I was stuck in traffic, unable to pull over.

I decided that Filthy didn't have another pub in him. I had to take what was left of him home. I drove down Carlisle Street, and stopped at the intersection with St Kilda Road in heavy traffic. Filthy was attempting to vomit out the rear passenger window. All of a sudden he went quiet. I turned around, thinking he might have just died.

Even though he was so pissed he could hardly scratch himself he was looking toward a car parked next to us. Filthy said, 'Have a look at this bloke. I don't like the look of him. What's his story? I don't look the like of him.'

The vehicle next to us was a late model Holden sedan. The driver was dressed in a suit, had short hair and looked like a middle-aged, typical businessman. But he looked at Filthy with a disgusted glare. Filthy glared back, but was too pissed to do it with meaning. I said, 'Don't worry about it Filthy, you're a citizen now, let it go.'

I thought this poor old Joe Citizen would die if he knew we were coppers.

As I started to drive off Filthy made his move. He couldn't stop and harass this driver so he did the next best thing. He spat a great big 'greenie' onto the middle of Joe Citizen's passenger side window.

I heard it land, and cringed as I turned and saw the disgusting blob slowly slide down the window. The target responded instantly.

This driver lifted his bum off the seat, pulled out his wallet and began to open it. All of us in the car knew what was coming – we had all done it many, many times. We knew he was not about to offer us money.

Just as we expected, he opened his wallet and flashed us a police badge. I saw my police career flash before me. Everyone thought he was an inspector or something, and urged me to just do a runner.

All of us in the car attempted to hide our faces, dropping low in the seat. Filthy let out a big, 'Oh Shit!' But the totally drunk Filthy was the only one to actually have a look at the badge. Filthy cried, 'Stop, stop! Look at the badge – it's bullshit.' I looked and noticed that the badge wasn't quite right. It was a fake.

Everyone stopped hiding their faces and actually looked at the badge. We all let out a cheer and started doing the badge shuffle, removing our badges from our rear jean pockets and simultaneously thrusting them at this wanker.

The wanker was so shocked he could barely drive across the intersection. He parked. We all managed to climb out of our little car. Tim, the youngest most-junior cop of us all, was ordered to be in charge of him.

Tim patted him down for weapons then removed his wallet, revealing the offensive fake badge. We were all laughing. I opened the rear passenger side door and lifted a towel lying on the back seat.

There, in front of me were a couple of hundred 'Buddha Sticks' – top quality cannabis all wrapped in aluminum foil, all tied up in bundles. Each bundle had a label attached with words like, 'DAVE $900' or 'STEVE $1,100.'

I called out for everyone to have a look at all this shit. It was all very amusing. We all started patting old Filthy on the back, saying things like, 'Why retire now, you're at your prime. Sensational.'

Filthy said, 'They don't teach that shit at the academy nowadays.' He looked at young Tim and said, 'Instincts, son – you need to trust your instincts.'

Tim handcuffed our catch. We started loading all the grass into our car. Darren then elected to drive Joe Citizen's car back to the station. Joe started saying, 'Excuse me' all the time. Everyone ignored him. I told him several times, 'You don't have to say anything, so shut up.'

As I started to put Joe in the back of our car he stopped,

again saying, 'Excuse me, sir.' I finally said, 'For Christ's sake, What?'

Joe said, 'I think you better have this.' He then turned and lifted the back of his suit jacket up and revealed a black leather holster containing a .38 six-shot revolver.

I ripped the gun out of the holster and pushed him face first against the car.

I opened the breech and emptied six live hollow-point rounds into my hand. Suddenly what seemed so hilarious wasn't. I looked at Tim. Looks can't kill, but guns can.

He said, 'But …' then thought better of it. I said in a very quiet serious voice, 'There's no but.' We got a cold shiver down our spines, realising we were all unarmed. I recall being more angry at Tim for missing the gun than I was at the crook for having it.

We took him back to our plainclothes office, then executed a search warrant on his home. It was a normal, well-kept place in suburbia but it was full of stolen goods and the roof was packed with hydroponically-grown marijuana. All up it was a great arrest – and from outside it looked like a text book operation. But we knew different.

At the very end of a very long day the four of us who were still awake opened cans of Fosters. We were in the first floor muster room. Filthy and Chooka were curled up asleep on the floor. Tim looked asleep at his desk, about four metres from us, his head down on his forearm, facing out the window.

He had been very upset with himself. I looked at the reflection in the window and saw that his eyes were open, and that he was far from sleeping. I walked over and tried to make him feel better.

I said, 'It could be worse, we could all be lying shot in the gutter.' Tim said, 'Yeah, thanks. I feel much better.' He didn't look it.

I said, 'Have a beer, we've all made mistakes – well, not as bad as yours. Like I've never nearly had my boss and all my work mates killed.'

Tim looked at me and smiled. He said, 'You're never serious, but you would never make a mistake like that.'

I touched him on the shoulder and said, 'Just learn from your mistakes. Always remember, when you do something, anything, do it one hundred percent or just don't do it at all. Policing is a very serious business, I just never take myself seriously when I do it.'

I felt sorry for the next poor bastard Tim searched.

DURING my undercover days I used to get right into it. I used to have to feel like a low life scum bag so I could act and look like one.

At this time I was convinced I had to act, but I wasn't acting, I was being a scum bag. You just can't act, it doesn't hold water.

Anyway, I had a set of clothes I would put on that would transform me mentally into what I was to become. I knew that if I believed I was a low-life heroin-using parasite, I could convince others I was one. So I developed a person that was between the normal Angus and disgusting Dean Collie. I would become Lex.

Lex was hip but not trendy, with-it but not cool. Imagine a 'Fonzie' from the series *Happy Days* with a bad hair cut and no cool. That was Lex.

I was Lex when I wanted to work undercover down The

Street. I could blow my cover as Lex without a problem. I did not have to protect him like I did Dean Collie. I needed Dean to keep in touch with The Street.

There were Lexes everywhere; they were a dime a dozen. He was the typical scum bag. I recall Lex wanted to wear the old blue and white check Miller Shirt with the silver thread in it, but I could never find my old shirts. Mum must have thrown them out. She always had good taste.

And, yes, Lex was known to wear an old pair of tight fitting black acid washed stretch jeans with the worn-out patch on the right side where he always scratched his balls. It's a bloke thing, you do it just to show people you've got them or something.

I would rub oil through my hair, wearing the same old jeans. And I would never, I mean never, wash the jeans. You can wear jeans for years and not wash them. The best part about it is they don't fade.

I found the downside was that when I got home from work my girlfriend wouldn't let me in the house. This meant I would arrive home after a hard day's work, ring the door bell and start to take all my clothes off on the front porch. My girlfriend would throw a towel at me, I would wrap the towel around me so the neighbours would not see all my 'rudie bits' and walk back inside.

I would then jump in a hot shower and wash The Street off – or try to. I think it was in the blood. But the warm water and soap could wash The Street out of my mind. It allowed me to be me. The problem was that I started to lose who me was. This never affected my police work as much as it did my social life. Now, years later, I realise that Lex, Dean and me were in fact all parts of the same person – no acting required.

I BELIEVE the difference between an also-ran detective and a good detective is massive. I believe if you're going to do a job, it's all or nothing. I tend to put my whole self into it. Sometimes it pays dividends and sometimes it gets me in the shit.

When you are an investigator,d 'avenues of inquiry' are the roads in which the investigation travels. For example, a crime happens, we then do door knocks, use the media to find suspects and maybe set up a police caravan at the crime scene. These are avenues of inquiry.

Being a cop is fantastic, being an investigating detective is even better. I got to live in my very own TV murder mystery, often without the murder but a mystery all the same. It is up to you to solve the case.

As an investigator often you are given a crime, and the easy part is finding out who did it. The hard part is finding a nexus between the crime and the offender.

Then you have to collect it in such a way as it can be used in evidence. Keep an open mind. Always look for 'avenues of inquiry.'

As the saying goes, 'The mind is like a parachute, it only works when it's open.'

chapter 10

IN THE DOCK

'I'd always wanted to be a hard bitten detective. Now I was'

I WAS working plainclothes duty with Darren one day when we got back to our office and found trouble. Our boss called a meeting and we were told we all had to be there. It could only be bad news.

The boss started by saying, 'A United States warship, believed to be nuclear powered, will dock at Station Pier in two days time. Due to intelligence received, we expect large demonstrations.

'The District Commander has directed that all leave and rest days have been cancelled forthwith. I don't care how you do it, but you will all be wearing full, yes full, uniform on Friday. You, of course, may choose to go off sick – saying your dog got run over, you have gonorrhoea, diarrhoea, your dick fell off or whatever – but in that case, as soon as you are fit to work, you will be in charge of the property office, brief book and buying lunches.

'Any questions?'

All quiet except for a few muffled mumblings.

The boss said, 'Dismissed,' and we were.

Friday rolled up and so did we. Some moustaches had to go

or were heavily trimmed, hair got cut, some just got heavily gelled and shoved under caps.

Uniforms were too small, too dirty, and often with belts and tie pins missing. Some of the black uniform issue shoes had been replaced with black privately purchased casual shoes. We looked a shambles – like rejects from *Police Academy*.

We were picked up at our office in a large bus and conveyed to the Port Melbourne Docks. We had all worked in plainclothes for so long we had gone a little feral and felt weird back in uniform.

I whispered to Darren, 'Don't look now but I think you're a Jack.'

THE pier was packed with screaming protesters. Our bus pushed its way through the mob and stopped after going through a large gate that closed behind us. After a while the Commander appeared to give the coach's address.

'We are here to protect our naval visitors from America. The issue is that the sailors have the right to come and go from their ship as they like.

'For the past two hours these protesters have not allowed free passage to and from this pier. We are here to remedy this situation. Listen to your sergeants. You are not to arrest anyone unless specifically directed by your sergeants. Listen to our commands and take care.'

The Commander strode off.

I took this to mean that this was serious shit and that shit was going to happen.

The upside was that we were looking forward to meeting some of the women protesters that gave the old Diggers such a hard time at an Anzac Day Parade a few weeks earlier.

Our lot was mixed in with about a hundred other real uniform police. I told Paul and Darren they better behave because there were cops everywhere. We tried to mingle but from the looks we got from the real cops it appeared they thought we might be enemy infiltrators.

Darren, Paul, Sandy and I did dag it up a bit, anyway. I had to produce my police badge three times to police who thought we didn't belong.

Paul looked the funniest. He was a very thick set boofheaded bloke with black hair and a large black droopy moustache. We called him the Turk as he looked exactly like a Turkish terrorist. Now he looked like a Turkish terrorist in a bodgie police uniform. No cops asked to see his ID because he looked too scary to approach.

We all found ourselves in the front line in this serious demonstration. The protesters were full on. Many of them very tough 'Women Against War' types. They really hated men full stop. Men in uniform tended to set them right off – the wrong way.

We stood there in a straight line stopping the protesters getting near the ship. In front of us, about one metre away were the protesters, all screaming things like, 'Fascist Pigs' etc. Right in front of me was a particularly annoying bongo drummer. I thought the piano accordion was bad.

This bloke had hair down to his bum and kept on hitting the drum making this senseless moronic tune, singing, 'Coppers are pigs, fascist pigs' on and on and on.

Every now and then he would pause to spit on me or another copper nearby. God it was hard to stand there being spat on.

I looked over to the Turk. I noticed even the protesters were keeping well away from him. Every time a protester got anywhere near him he peeled back his lips and snarled, then they would melt back into the crowd.

As a police officer you realise that they are not attacking you personally, so you don't take it personally. You just turn the other cheek and smile. You don't take sides, you just do your job. Insults are water off a duck's back.

I whispered to Darren, 'Pass the word, the bongo drummer is mine – don't touch the bongo drummer.'

I then started to try to work out how I was going to shove the bongo drum up his arse. I was getting really pissed off at several other cops that also thought they could have the bongo drummer. I said, 'Don't even think about it. He's mine.'

As the spittle dripped down my shirt he just kept smiling, spitting, drumming and teasing, totally unaware of the imminent extreme violence planned against him.

I was prepared to overlook and ignore several other extremely annoying bastards just to get the drummer. I knew I would have to fight several other cops to do it, but that was a small price to pay for revenge. Not that I was taking it personally or anything.

This drummer was smarter than I gave him credit for. As our superiors started to give us orders to attack, sorry, I mean walk forward and calmly and safely clear the pier of protesters, the bongo drummer did a runner. He stayed out of my reach as the 'clear the pier' order was given.

I had almost got to him when he wisely leapt off the pier into deep cold water, definitely safer than having a close encounter with an enraged copper. The cunning, wet bastard.

A short time later a very careful observer would have seen

a particularly nasty protester get led along by an angry policeman, the policeman bending her arm up her back in an effort to control her. The arm bent too far and went in a direction arms weren't meant to. The policeman immediately let go and pretended it didn't happen. He then picked another target.

After several battles won and lost the cops were given the order to go home. A senior officer walked up to our bus as we were getting onto it. He said, 'I want four volunteers to stay till eleven so the night shift can take over.' I was right in his face. I tried to turn away but there was nowhere to hide.

No volunteers put their hands up so the officer said, 'You, you, you and you, report to the gatehouse now. Thanks for your assistance.' A sergeant unknown to us, Darren, Sandy and me were it.

When we got to the gatehouse, it was raining and the pier was totally deserted. The odd US sailor came and went, but there were no protesters. We sat there watching ourselves on the late news, cheering as the police did the big 'charge'. I even got a glimpse of the bongo drummer as he dived off the pier to safety.

All the navy sailors had passed and walked through the gate by themselves. A short time later I heard an, 'excuse me officer.' I looked out the window and saw a women with her daughter. Her daughter was about eighteen years old and attractive.

The mother explained to me that her daughter had met a lovely sailor and wanted to visit him before he left. I started to telephone the ship, but I paused for a moment when I thought I heard a distant bongo drum. I did, I did hear a bongo drum.

It was like being in the jungle waiting for the savages to attack except when we heard the unforgettable words, 'Coppers are pigs, fascist pigs,' again and again. We put up with it for a minute or so until he started to get into the face of the young girl and her mother. He then started singing new disgusting little songs aimed at them.

I looked at my sergeant, the look said, 'please?' The sergeant, who I didn't know, was clearly a wise and decent man. He said, 'He's yours, go.'

I immediately looked away, uninterested, in an attempt to catch him off guard. Then I turned and leapt head first out the large open counter window.

The bongo man might have been a tuneless idiot, but he could recognise danger when he saw it, particularly when it dived through a window at him. He was off, straight up the pier with me running full bore after him.

He maintained about a three metre lead on me for the length of the pier then he turned right and headed for an old deserted house.

As he got close he yelled out for help, but I didn't care as I knew it was deserted. Just as he got to the front of the house I leapt, grabbing a handful of hair. I came to the ground knocking over several large tins of paint. One paint tin was pink oil paint, it opened, we rolled in the paint as he struggled to get away.

Bongo yelled, 'Help!' Knowing there was no-one to save him I yelled, 'Help!', mocking him.

I yelled, 'Help, Help!' even louder than he was yelling. Of course, no-one came. After all the abuse, all the spitting, he was finally mine. It was one of those moments when it was great to be a peacekeeper.

Then the front door of the dark deserted house opened, and about twenty 'Women Against War' ran at me screaming. This was not good. Bongo Man must have belonged to them.

I wrapped one hand around his long hair and hung on. The women kicked, poked, scratched and spat on me. With my one free hand I tried to keep them back, then I realised I was in trouble. I was losing badly and getting hurt.

My free hand then started to punch these women as hard as it could, I recall even poking one of the she devils in the eye to get her to let go. These were desperate times.

Until now I had never hit a woman in my life, but this was no time for chivalry. They were using their feet, fists, nails and teeth against me. It was like being attacked by a pack of wild dogs, although the dogs would have smelled better.

I'd always wanted to be a hard bitten detective. Now I was.

Through the women I saw two large American sailors who could see what was happening. They could not intervene as this could cause a diplomatic incident. I couldn't have cared less – I was in serious trouble. I wish they would have nuked the bitches. One of the sailors ran back toward the gatehouse to get me help, the other stayed.

At one stage I got to my police radio, curled up and screamed, 'End of Princes Pier, urgent! I'm in trouble!' A woman grabbed the radio from me, pushed the button and screamed, 'No he's not, we'll look after him.' That was against the rules.

Bongo Man was in agony, he was screaming at the women to stop and to let me go. I had so much of his hair in my hand that it wouldn't pull out. If it did his whole scalp would come off. He just wanted the whole thing to stop.

Eventually several other cops came and jumped in, then

cop cars screamed up. They got to me and Bongo. By this stage Bongo and I were stuffed. Someone cuffed Bongo Man. It wasn't me – I didn't have the strength.

I staggered to my feet, sore all over, badly scratched and bruised with the makings of a black eye swelling already. Several other police were assaulted by the women as they arrived. I staggered forward and grabbed one of the women that had been 'up close and personal' throughout the attack, she was still screaming abuse. She was one of many that assaulted me, but was the only one that I could identify.

The rest of the women retired back into the dark, undeserted house. As we drove away I heard over the radio that several cops were missing equipment such as police caps. The women must have taken them into the house.

They joked about who was going back in there to get them. No-one was game.

I was taken to hospital to have my injuries checked. As I was taken into casualty the nurses thought I had been ripped apart by a lion. I was happy to stick to that story.

But Darren, my trusted and loyal mate, opened his big mouth and told them it was a bunch of women. The nurses thought that was hilarious, so did the doctors, cops, cleaners, patients and any other bastard that happened to be passing by.

Darren told me they had arrested and charged four of the women that had attacked me. They gave Bongo Man a heap of charges too. He also said they had got statements from the mother and daughter at the gatehouse. I would have smiled if it didn't hurt so much. I slept and was actually off work for three days.

I carried the classic female scratch marks for two weeks, four deep scratches about a centimetre apart down the right side of my face. They were the worst injuries I got in sixteen years in the job.

ONE afternoon I was with Darren working plainclothes and we were doing what we loved – hunting crooks in The Street. It was getting dark when we saw the divvie van pull up near The Cafe. Then Helen and Simon, two uniform cops, got out and sat in the caf to have a smoke and a coffee.

Now how are we meant to catch crooks with them around? I wanted them to piss off, they made The Street nervous. I then saw something that could brighten our day.

We walked over the road to the post office where Morrie had just staggered out of the phone box. He was in his fifties, totally pissed and very angry at the world. Sober or drunk he would be shadow boxing the whole time, ducking and weaving non-existent punches.

Morrie had just got out of prison two weeks earlier after doing a twenty-two year stretch for armed robbery and murder. His body wasn't used to alcohol so just a few drinks made him blind drunk. He was short and stocky with a flat face and nose. Twenty-two years in prison made his language disgusting.

He scared the shit out of the general public and it was our duty to protect them.

We walked up to Morrie, told him we were police and that he was under arrest. He thought that was great, he had someone to fight. He was swinging punches at me but we were able to lead him over to the back of the police van. I opened the door and we only just managed to get him inside. He went off his head when we closed the back door and locked it.

We quickly disappeared and took up our our surveillance position again. We laughed as we could see the van rocking wildly. After a couple of minutes the van became still. Morrie had fought his three rounder and was asleep again.

Simon and Helen casually walked up to their van. Now, Simon was a very serious cop, with short red hair, freckles and a short temper. He was the sort of cop that talked tough because he wasn't. Helen was tall and thin, immaculately presented and looked more like a beauty consultant.

Darren and I left our surveillance post and walked to The Street. As they got into the van and closed the doors I said, 'Shhhh'. They were directly opposite us as they began to drive off. We were both laughing. They closed their doors. Simon gave way to one car and pulled out into heavy traffic. Just as he did that Morrie woke, screamed at the top of his voice and smashed the inside of the van.

Simon slammed on the brakes, then Batman and Robin dived out of the van and took cover behind their bonnet. Simon drew his gun and screamed, 'Who are you?' He must have thought he was in the *X Files*.

It was funny to see two cops approach the back of their own van, guns drawn, as if they expected a lion to jump out of it. Morrie was going crazy, the van was rocking, and he was not listening to any of their demands. Traffic built up around them, and a crowd gathered. The crowd wondered why the cops didn't know who was in the back of their van.

Simon was very upset and angry. He screamed, 'What are you doing in our van? Why are you in there?' Finally Simon got up enough guts to put his face to the window and peep inside. Simon recognised Morrie and started to abuse him.

We had moved position. Simon decided that he didn't care

how he got in the van, he was taking him to jail. As they drove up The Street I waved to Helen. I think my cheeky grin gave me away. She screamed to Simon, 'Look at Angus, it was him. That bastard!' It looked as if she was trying to get Simon to stop the car to abuse me – or shoot me, maybe.

We went back to protecting the public.

I ARRIVED at the Prahran Magistrates' Court. Two of the women arrested on the night of the bongo drummer incident had pleaded not guilty to assault and other charges. One of the women I knew nothing about, as someone else had arrested her. The other one was the one that was up close and personal, attacking me to force me to let go of Bongo Man. I walked into court and saw the two women. You couldn't miss them – they didn't look like social workers or barristers or even hookers. They had a look all of their own.

It was a beautiful day and I was in a hurry to knock off early to go fishing. The prosecutor told me the women were up first, then stood up and called the defendant's name. The defendant walked forward and sat behind her barrister. The prosecutor then bellowed, 'I call the informant.'

That was my cue. I stood up and marched into the witness box. The magistrate nodded to me as I gave my full name and the oath.

I gave my evidence in the usual way. Well, then it started. The barrister was most upset with me. He accused me of lying to the court, misleading the court, fabricating evidence, exaggerating. He disagreed with everything I said, as usual. The defendant seated behind him was saying under her breath, 'Lying male bastard, prick, Nazi.' Twice her own barrister had to tell her to shut up.

I told the court how she had spat on me, kicked me, scratched me, poked me in the eyes, and taken my police radio. Eventually it was over. The magistrate obviously believed me and understood what a difficult job the police had to contend with. The magistrate had read the statements of the mother and daughter, as it was the same beak who had heard the guilty plea from the Bongo Man the day before.

I sat back down in the court waiting for his decision. He convicted and fined her about $500, a good result all around. I was about to leave when the prosecutor stood up and called the next case, he called the defendant's name, then he said, 'I call the informant.'

I looked over to another copper named Scotty who had his head in his hands peeping at me through his fingers. Something was terribly wrong. He just shook his head at me.

I could not work out what he was on about. I stood up about to leave when the prosecutor said, 'I call Constable Angus.'

My heart stopped, I looked at the prosecutor. I thought this could not be happening. It was true. I had got up out of my seat and into the witness box so fast Scotty had missed out. I looked at Scotty, who just shook his head again.

I had just given evidence against the wrong defendant. No wonder the barrister and the defendant were abusing me so much. I reluctantly got back into the witness box and swore myself in. My mind was running at a hundred miles an hour. What could I do?

I couldn't just say, 'Okay, time out, excuse me everyone, I just gave evidence for the last hour against the wrong person.' Especially when the magistrate had just convicted her.

I did the only thing possible in the circumstances. I gave very similar evidence to the previous case. Surely a little bit more bullshit wouldn't matter. I peeped at Scotty who was, by this stage, almost under his seat. From the corner of my eye I saw Scotty almost crawl out of the court, not wanting to have anything to do with me or what was happening. The police prosecutor had a strange perplexed look on his face, as did the magistrate. I danced around in the witness box again for a while. My evidence was nowhere near as good as the first time.

But it was good enough. She was convicted. I ran from the court. I found Scotty lurking in some bushes out the front.

He said, 'What happened?'

I said, 'Guilty, $600 fine. They shouldn't look so much alike.'

He said, 'Their names don't look alike, you idiot.' He had a point.

Anyway, I'd protected the public enough for one day. I went fishing to recover.

chapter 11

PICKING UP CHICKS

'Maybe he was just giving it a cuddle'

IT was a public holiday and The Street was deserted, except for a few die-hard addicts looking to die the hard way, as most eventually do. There was a call for a police unit to do a job, but all the other St Kilda units were busy.

Darren picked up the radio and said, 'St Kilda 450, we'll do that job for you.' The D24 operator said, 'Thanks 450. Your job is a "story to tell." Mrs Adams Flat 19/36 Milton Street, Elwood.' Darren responded: 'Roger that, 24102.' (We always had to give our registered number when we took a job.)

We pulled up out the front of a four-storey block of flats and walked to the top floor. We knocked politely and the door was opened by a lovely old lady who said, 'Come in.'

I said in my best official voice, 'What seems to be the problem?'

She said, 'Well it's terrible really. The problem is chicken noises. Now, chickens can make a lot on noise, especially when they get clucky – you know, when they sit on the eggs. I used to have chickens as I child when I lived in the country.'

Well, off she went with her life story, well away from the problem at hand. She was putting the chicken before the egg so to speak.

I interrupted her and said, 'Just contact the body corporate. I'm sure your neighbours are not allowed to have chickens in the building.' I wasn't sure as I was not up on chicken legislation, but it sounded right.

She said, 'No, not in this building, over there.'

She led us over to her kitchen window. 'I was doing the dishes here with the window open. I heard the noise so I looked out down to that house there, see that house with the chicken coop, and there he was, he had his pants down doing a terrible thing to that chicken.'

She then pointed to a chicken that was lying motionless on the ground within the cage. It looked well and truly stuffed. She went on to say she rang the police because she thought, 'That poor chicken.'

I looked at Darren, who was silently mouthing the word, 'Chicken'.

I said, 'You saw a man actually doing something to that chicken right there.' I pointed to the only motionless chicken in the pen. She said, 'Oh it was terrible, when he finished he put it back in the pen and it hasn't moved since.' I wasn't surprised.

I said, 'How many men live in that house?'

The respectable old lady said, 'Only one, his name is Eric. I thought he was a lovely man, he helped me when I had a fall back in January. It was Eric with the chicken. My hearing's not too good, but my eye sight is perfect.'

I informed her that I would need a statement, but we wouldn't do it at that moment. Darren and I left quietly –

we were on the case. On the way down the stairs Darren said, 'Maybe he was just giving it a cuddle.' He was always an optimist.

I said, 'I'm not a pheasant plucker, I'm a pheasant plucker's son and I'm only plucken pheasants while the pheasant pluckers gone.'

Darren walked along saying, 'Chicken?' over and over again. That was the great thing about being a copper, every day was different.

We knocked on the suspect's door. The door opened. An attractive woman said, 'Hello' in a cheerful voice.

This made me take a step backwards. For some reason I didn't think a chicken fucker would have a girlfriend or a wife, but you always should have an open mind. Parachutes and all that.

We identified ourselves. Her name was Sue. We walked inside. It was a lovely house. I asked to see Eric. She said, 'Certainly, I think he's out the back. I'll just get him.' I motioned for Darren to look at the wedding photo on the wall. There were no chickens in the wedding party. In fact, no poultry was visible at all.

Moments later Sue introduced us to Eric. They both seemed quite happy and intrigued to know why we were there. I told Sue we just might go out into the backyard to talk with Eric.

Sue wanted to know what was wrong, but she eventually left us. As she was leaving I asked her if she had been home all morning. Sue said that she had, but she went out shopping for a little while. I asked Eric what he did for a job. He was an executive in a large accounting firm.

I asked, 'Fond of chickens, are you Eric?'

He said, 'What's this about?' He started to get shitty, and looked like he was about to panic.

I said, 'Come over here.' We walked to the chicken coop. I pointed to the dead chicken lying on the ground.' I said, 'What happened to that chicken?'

He said, 'It's dead. Chickens die all the time.'

I said, 'It looks fucked.' With that Eric went right off tap. He demanded we leave his home immediately, threatening to get his solicitors onto us.

I grabbed him and forced him face first against the wire. I put the handcuffs on.

I said, 'Well, we could have done this nicely, but it's your choice. You're under arrest for having sex with and killing this chicken. The charge is bestiality.'

He turned and whispered, 'It's my chicken.'

I corrected him, 'Was your chicken.'

We walked Eric through the house. Sue demanded to know what was going on and almost started fighting us. She screamed that her husband had done nothing. She saw the dead chicken I was holding. She then screamed, 'Why are you taking my husband and that chicken?'

I said, 'I'm terribly sorry, but it's evidence.'

She said, 'Evidence? Evidence? What evidence?'

We took Eric out to the car, but Sue was still demanding to know what was going on. We put him in the back seat. I looked at Eric and said, 'Well, this is going to test the relationship.'

He closed his eyes and dropped his head. I put the chicken in the boot and walked back to Sue. I felt like I was about to deliver a death message.

I said, 'Sue, your husband is under arrest for having sex

with a chicken'. Her face just dropped and she said, 'You're not serious. Sex?'

I said, 'While you were out shopping a person up in those flats saw him pay a visit to the chicken coop, and do the business with the chicken. The chicken went berserk and died.'

She said, 'You're kidding. How can he have sex with a chicken. It's impossible?'

I said, 'I think that's why it's dead.'

Sue started to put it all together in her mind. She said, 'I found one of our other chickens dead last Saturday and I couldn't work out why. Eric loved those chickens. Well, you know what I mean.' I could see Sue thinking.

I said, 'We'll take Eric to the St Kilda Police Station.'

She said, 'You can take Eric wherever you like, I don't want him. How am I going to tell my friends about this. A chicken? He prefers a chicken? Christ, what do I tell mum?'

I was lost for words. Sue finished up by saying, 'You blokes, a crack in the concrete isn't safe.' She put me in the same basket as the chicken fucker. I was a touch offended. She pretended to talk to her mum, 'Hello mum. Oh everything's fine, Eric's just been arrested for rooting one of our chickens – the cops took my chicken for evidence.' She then walked off. All in all, I thought she took it pretty well.

In the car and back at the station Eric was being a real prick. It was a bad mistake. The whole station had to come and see what a chicken fucker looked like. A lot of chicken jokes flew around. Sandy said, 'Angus, you'd have killed a few chickens in your time, I reckon.'

Whilst we were interviewing Eric, the wife was at home getting over the shock of it all. Not.

I heard over the radio the fire brigade had been called to a fire in Milton Street. Sue had lit a bonfire on her front lawn. I walked back into the interview room and told Eric, and he sat there shaking his head. I said to Eric sympathetically, 'You fuck just one chicken.'

Eric pleaded guilty. The court heard how this stupid act had cost him his job and his marriage. Sue had telephoned his work, his friends, even the press. The press loved it.

A woman once said, 'Women need a reason, men just need a place.'

Anyway.

chapter 12

JUMPER LEADS

**'The boss preferred not to know.
He was smart like that'**

IT was a cold winter's day. I was working as a detective one morning when a Mr Philips, aged about sixty, came into the station. He was talking of a person named Timothy.

He said Timothy was a con man, about thirty five years old and he had a set of stolen number plates in his office. All he knew was that the number plates were stolen. He knew nothing else. This bloke seemed to really hate this Timothy, so I had to be careful as it might well have been a domestic situation. He said Timothy was smooth.

As a cop you never believe one side of the story. I didn't know either person so I decided to pay Timothy a visit. His limousine company was nearby, so I walked down there by myself. I walked into a plush foyer and spoke to the receptionist. I told her who I was. She telephoned Timothy and then said I could go upstairs. At the top of the stairs was a large, beautifully-furnished office.

Timothy stood up and shook my hand. I was impressed. He was about six foot one, immaculately dressed in a $1000 Italian suit. He didn't have a hair out of place, spoke with an educated voice and oozed class.

I felt I had to stand a little taller and pronounce my words carefully. I attempted to match his class. I could now see why it was Timothy and not Tim.

I sat at the huge desk. I said, 'I've received information suggesting you have a set of stolen number plates in your office.'

He said, 'I would say that a Mr Philips has come to you recently. I sacked him two days ago. I'm sure you understand he is upset, but business is business.

'He was a driver of mine. I had to let him go. He has a drinking problem.'

I said, 'I see. He suggested to me that your business is in dire trouble.'

Timothy: 'We have bad times but you battle on.' He then told me that he was very busy and that he had to attend to business. I thought obviously Mr Philips was trying to use me to get back at Timothy. I started to leave, we shook hands again. I apologised for any inconvenience.

As I walked out of his office Timothy said, 'Detective.' I paused and turned back to face him. He said, 'I know it's cold outside but take my advice, if you're going to wear a suit, wear a suit'.

He waved his right hand in an up and down motion. He continued, 'That jumper just doesn't suit.'

I smiled and said, 'Yes, I suppose you're right.'

He said, 'I am. It's the first thing I noticed as you walked in the room. That is a fisherman's knit jumper – keep it for fishing or some such thing.'

I said, 'Thanks for the advice and I am terribly sorry to have caused you or your staff any inconvenience. I won't bother you again.' I left.

I walked down the stairs and left the building. Tim had been doing well until he mentioned my jumper. It was my favourite; my mum had knitted it.

By the time I got back to my office, I was furious. I mumbled away as I typed out a search warrant based on the information from the extremely reliable, totally truthful, never ever wrong employee of the year, Mr Philips.

I asked our receptionist, Deb, what she thought of my jumper. She agreed it was lovely. So there. I gathered a posse together and we all walked to see Mr Fashion Plate. I told everyone his name was Tim.

Six of us walked in. I placed the search warrant on the receptionist's table. I said, 'Hello, I'm back, please stay seated.'

I walked straight up stairs. No Tim. Or Timothy.

I immediately started searching his office. Next to his seat at his desk was a loaded double barrel 'Purdy' shotgun. This is a hand made, top of the range, work-of-art gun.

I had checked if he had gun licence. He didn't. I admired it as I made it safe. I said to Darren, 'Tim must have other enemies besides me. He may have insulted somebody else's dress sense.'

While we were searching I found the receptionist talking to Tim on the blower, then hanging up. After a while it became obvious Tim was not coming back because Timmy knew what we would find.

We found that he had written about two hundred valueless cheques and re-financed two Mercs worth about $120,000 each.

He had taken out a loan for $120,000 to buy a car, then changed the number plates and took out another loan to buy the same car. Totally illegal. So I had him for theft of $240,000 plus the value of all the valueless cheques he had written and an unlicensed shotgun. I was happy – and nice and warm in my jumper.

We left the building with boxes of paperwork. Some I didn't need, but I took them just to upset him.

We checked every address known to man. No Tim. From receipts, I found that he had a Qantas Gold Card and regularly flew all over Australia to play in the casinos. The bastard disappeared. I had four days to go, then I was on leave. I was going fishing interstate with my jumper so I needed to catch him soon.

His ex-wife contacted me. She was stunning. She cried in my office as she told me the story of how her parents had gone guarantor in a big business deal Tim did. Result: they lost their big house in Brighton.

She told me Tim would be very hard to find. He was smart and would not put himself in a position to go to jail. What I needed was a cunning plan.

I turned my mind to locating him. I thought 'avenues of inquiry' – where would he absolutely have to go? I located a post office box where he got some of his mail sent. I went to that post office and looked in the box. There were several large cheques made out for cash. I knew Tim would be busting to get them. A man who dressed so well couldn't live without a large cash flow for long.

I got the surveillance 'dogs' (crime surveillance unit) to work for me for one day. It was now my last day before leave. I was desperate. I got the dogs to sit off the post office box, his parent's place and the casino.

I had nowhere else to look. At lunch time I got a telephone

call. He said, 'Hello, I'm barrister Simon Fortesque of Fortesque and Briggs, I'm acting on behalf of my client Timothy. What is your current situation regarding him?'

I said vaguely, 'Timothy? I know that name. Oh, Timothy, of course. Well, as you know I executed a search warrant at his business premises and he wasn't there.

'Can you inform him that I am extremely sorry for the embarrassment both professionally and personally that I have caused him. My superiors would like to apologise on my behalf for my incorrect assessment of offences that I thought he had committed.'

He said, 'Well, I should think so, Timothy is highly regarded and I am astounded at your behaviour.'

I then went on to tell the barrister that I needed to return all the documents to him as soon as possible as I wasn't interested in civil matters.

I said, 'I am a detective. We only deal with criminal matters, so please apologise to him. He was right. I should never have listened to Mr Philips. Although I do have a shotgun belonging to him, and he is unlicensed, please wait whilst I check my diary.'

I pretended to look up dates. I said, 'Well, I'm busy this week but how about 2.30pm next Wednesday at my office'. He said, 'So you do not wish to speak to my client now.'

I said, 'Yes, I do, next Wednesday at 2.30pm. Can you call me back to confirm that appointment?'

He said, 'So, that's it then. You don't wish to speak to my client now?'

I said, 'No, I would appreciate a call back to confirm next Wednesday.'

He said, 'Certainly.'

I put the phone down. Just as I started to think about what I had just done the phone rang. It was Tim.

I said, 'Hello, Timothy, I'm terribly sorry about everything.' Timothy was on the attack. He said, 'Well, I have spoken to my barrister and we are very upset about how you have handled this inquiry. It was only ever civil. You have completely embarrassed me both professionally and privately.'

I said, 'I would appreciate it if you could come and sort the unlicensed firearm out next week.' He agreed and hung up the phone.

I immediately telephoned the leader of the surveillance team.

I said, 'Smurf, it's Angus, just bullshitted my tits off to Tim and his barrister. He's on his mobile and should be there any minute to pick up his money.'

I put the phone down and walked into the boss's office. The boss looked at me and said, 'What? I can tell you've done something wrong.' He was a trained detective.

I said, 'No, boss. We're about to catch Tim. It's just that I did something – "wrong" is a bit harsh – I think naughty is the word.'

The boss really wanted Tim arrested as we were going to charge him with about three hundred cheque offences. The only thing the boss was interested in was the crime figures. It's the 'Clean Up Rate' that counts.

Darren walked into the boss's office and said, 'Excuse me, Angus, the dogs just grabbed him. He double parked his Porsche outside the post office, he was arrested at his mail box. They'll be here in two minutes.'

I said, 'Fantastic, what about his Porsche.'

Darren said, 'That might take a bit longer. Smurf's driving it back here.' Probably via Sydney, I thought to myself.

I said, 'Boss, please remember, whatever happens I'm just protecting the community.'

The boss looked perplexed. I left. The boss preferred not to know. He was smart like that.

Moments later, Tim appeared. He was led into an interview room. I had a huge smile. I was happy, he looked sad.

I uncuffed him and sat him down. I could see and hear Tim's teeth grind with anger. I waited for him to speak. Nothing.

I said, 'G'day Tim, got anything to say about my jumper now?'

He said, 'You lied.'

I said, 'Correct.' At least we knew where we stood. I read out the full formal caution to him.

One of the other officers had put his wallet and his mobile phone on the interview room table. Tim picked it up and started to ring someone. I went to take it from him. He snatched it away and said, 'How dare you touch my phone, I am not a criminal.'

I stood there, smiled and said, 'Watch this.'

I walked to the interview room door and said, 'I can go in.' I stepped into the room. Then I said 'I can go out' and I stepped out. I repeated this several times. I walked over to Tim and removed the phone from his hand. I said, 'You can only go in.' I walked out.

Darren then told me that a barrister by the name of Fortesque was in with the boss. He was more upset than Tim. Darren and I organised the paperwork and the charges.

I had already got our secretary to type up all the charges,

three hundred and two in all. The total sum of the deceptions was over two million dollars, once you added the cheque offences together.

He had stolen so much from so many people it was amazing. He would write out a cheque and receive top of the range hotel accommodation, furniture, car hire and repair, clothing – you name it. He had the gift of the gab and a fantastic ability to impress people. After all, he was always well-dressed.

We charged and remanded him into custody. Mr Fortesque appeared at the remand hearing and treated me with total contempt.

He said, 'You lied to me, causing me to tell your lie to Timothy. This is the most unprofessional act I have come across.'

I said, 'It's no offence to lie, and I'll do it again if it protects the public from blood sucking leeches like your client, plus I have to go away fishing tomorrow.' I left. Timothy remained in custody for two weeks while he arranged a large surety for bail. At the County Court Tim got a huge fine and a long community based order. At least he tasted jail.

What I did was naughty, not wrong. And I don't regret it.

EARLY in our plainclothes days we decided to go up to the snow for a weekend – well, a Saturday night actually, then come home Sunday. Darren, Sandy, Paul and I drove up to Mt Hotham. We planned to do a bit of skiing but it was mainly a drinking-bonding session. At the end of skiing we ended up at a nightclub. We were all having a great time.

Darren was a dolphin trainer, I was a deep sea diver maintaining the telecommunication cable between Tasmania and the mainland – scraping the abalone of the cable, stuff like that. Sandy was a solicitor, Paul went one better, as a senior barrister. We spun bullshit to women most of the night.

The dolphin trainer brought his young lady home. She was about twenty or so, still at uni doing an arts degree. Home was a large 'A' frame house on the edge of a huge gully. We had great views.

Unfortunately, Darren was sleeping in my room. I stayed up for a while and eventually had to go to bed. As I tried to get to sleep I could hear them giggling. I put a pillow over my head and fell asleep.

I woke to a heap of yelling and screaming. I climbed out of bed to see what it was. I looked across the lounge and through the large glass windows. The young woman Darren had brought home was stark naked, standing on the thin rail of the balcony threatening to jump. It was snowing hard and freezing cold. Darren was pleading with her to get down. I screamed at him, 'What's her problem.'

He looked at me and said, 'I told her I was a cop.'

She screamed, 'I slept with a cop! I hate cops, cops killed my father.'

By this time Sandy and Paul were up too, asking questions. She had nothing more to live for, so it was goodbye cruel world. She covered her eyes and leapt off the balcony. We ran forward to see where she was going to land. Fortunately she landed in a deep snow drift. Darren was in shock. He thought he had caused her death. I told him he should never blow his cover.

She was perfectly all right. Sandy gave her a hot shower and she went home.

We all stayed up and drank. It was a lot safer.

ONE morning Darren came to work late. He missed the weekly meeting, the whole meeting stopped as he entered the room. When it finished I asked what happened. He said, 'I got booked for speeding – ninety in a sixty zone.'

I said, 'Didn't you flash Freddie?' Freddie being the police badge. Darren said, 'I think I was trumped. Have a look who gave it to me.'

It was the signature of the Chief Commissioner, S. I. Miller. Sensational. We jumped in the car and took it to straight to a picture framer, and waited until it was framed. It looked great. He then paid the fine.

Darren decided it wouldn't be a good career move putting the chief in the witness box to contest it.

THE problem with being a heroin addict is that you're a crook and you have to rely on other crooks to give you the heroin. The industry is full of criminals. Everyone that touches it are crooks, right up until it is either used by crooks or seized by police. Dirty, smelly, stupid, treacherous crooks.

They finally get enough money together to buy their daily dose of heroin. Even though the opium resin was collected by filthy rotten criminals who wouldn't wash their hands, sold to more filthy criminals working in an unclean clandestine laboratory mixing it with toxic chemicals while turning it into heroin.

It's then been up two arseholes, a stomach and a couple of fannies, then sold to you by a bloke that kept it in his mouth. It's good shit so they can't wait to whack it up their arm no matter where it's been.

I WAS working plainclothes down The Street one day and,

when I was buying lunch, I heard some screaming and crying. It was coming from a female toilet in McDonalds. I found a young women crying over a body.

The corpse had a familiar face. It was Josie, a young street kid turned prostitute. I checked her pulse, nothing. A syringe stuck out of one arm.

As the ambulance took her away one of the officers told me it was the third death that day in the St Kilda area. I took the survivor back to our police station. She was off her face on heroin and didn't make much sense.

She told me through her heroin stupor that they bought the gear from a black bloke named Norman. We left her to straighten up. Darren and I went hunting.

I saw Cindy hanging around the Caf. I double parked. She saw me coming and tried to slink off, but I grabbed her and searched her handbag. Hidden in the lining was a foil of heroin. She swore and carried on. I cuffed her and put her in the back seat. Darren and I drove off.

As we were driving I smiled and threw a cuff key over my shoulder onto Cindy's lap. Cindy had to spread her legs to allow the key to fall on the seat then squirmed around to grab the key and uncuff herself.

While she did this she was abusing me, muttering, 'You arrest me for an offence, that will be the day.'

I threw the foil I had said I found back to her. She opened it up. It was empty. She said, 'Christ!'

I dropped my voice to a serious tone. 'Cindy, do you know a new bloke, a black guy named Norman?'

She said, 'Am I a dog (informer). Do I look like a dog?' I didn't answer.

But she realised that I had never asked her for information

before. She suddenly became serious and said, 'What's wrong?' I said, 'It's Josie, she's left The Street and won't be coming back.'

Cindy knew there was only one way you leave The Street. She didn't say a word and just looked out the window. Tears welled in her eyes. One rolled down her face onto her lips. She said, 'When I was a little girl I used to think tears were salty to stop me crying.'

I stopped at a red light. In a different voice, Cindy said 'Leave your phone on.' She stepped out of our car and walked off. About fifteen minutes later she rang me and said, 'Where do you want him?'

I had thought of a cunning plan. To avoid Cindy having to give evidence I arranged for her to get Norman to do the deal in the driveway to her units. There was a large gate half-way up the driveway. She does the deal on the outside of the gate, we wait on the inside, see and hear the deal through a hole in the gate and arrest him.

Half an hour later Darren and I waited for the deal to take place and a little while later Cindy was waiting in her driveway. All of a sudden a motorbike pulled up in the driveway. Cindy looked back at us, as she knew there was nothing she could do.

It was Norman. Wearing the matching, colour co-ordinated full leathers and helmet. Norman was trendy, on a brand new racing CBR 500 motorbike. She reluctantly did the deal, and he drove off. We were on foot. It wasn't even worth us trying to arrest him. Norman was supposed to be on foot. At least we saw him.

Cindy was upset that he got away. I reassured her that she did a great job, that we got a look at him. I took the heroin she bought and thanked her. We drove off with our foil of heroin for testing at the Forensic Science Laboratory.

I met with Sue the scientist and told her the story that we expected it to be very high quality because we believed this Norman guy was responsible for heroin deaths.

She tested it, and it was pure, top quality, one hundred percent sugar. I knew we must have the wrong bloke. But selling Cindy sugar purporting it to be heroin is trafficking heroin. That's case law. I then wondered if there could be two Normans, both black, one trafficking heroin and the other sugar in St Kilda. Surely not?

We went back down The Street. We were very disappointed and still had no idea who he was. The motorbike registration came up as 'unknown' on the computer data base.

We thought even if we see him how the hell do you stop or catch a motorbike? We parked our car in Lock Street, just off Fitzroy Street, and walked up the road.

We had driven around looking for him for ages, then decided to have a break. Sure enough we heard the unmistakable sound of Norman's motorbike coming up the road toward us. Darren said, 'Shit, you're kidding.' We both turned and, sure enough, it was Norman.

I walked onto the edge of the roadway and looked toward Norman. He was accelerating up the road toward me. As he drew close I reached down and grabbed my imaginary heavy fishing line and lifted it to head height and pulled it tight. I braced myself ready to take off Norm's head.

He saw my actions and panicked. He ducked, slammed his brakes on skidding along the road to a stop. I started to laugh and mimic Norman's actions.

I pretended to be riding a motorbike trying to avoid the

imaginary line. Darren just stood there. Norman realised I was only joking, he then accelerated straight at me, skidded on the grass nature strip, kicked the stand down on his bike, stepped off and strode straight at me. Norman was pissed off.

I smiled and stepped backwards holding both hands in the air obviously surrendering. Norman was wearing a black full face helmet with the visor down. I couldn't see his face, but I suspect he would have looked cross. I backed up to a fence and stopped. Norman brought back his fist about to punch me right in the face. As he got to an arm's length I ripped out my little Saturday night special .38 calibre revolver and smashed it straight into his helmet just below his visor. The visor lifted just enough for my whole hand and the snub-nosed gun to disappear into his helmet.

My hand was so far into the helmet that my gun must have been in his mouth – or his eye socket.

I said in a very loud voice, 'Can you hear me?' The helmet nodded. I said, 'You are under arrest for trafficking heroin, so shut up.' He lay down, I turned to Darren and said, 'You got cuffs?' He stepped forward and cuffed him. I only ever had cuffs or keys, never both.

I said, 'Do they still teach that arrest procedure at the academy?' Darren said, 'I must have been sick that day'. He then said, 'I can't wait to read your statement.'

Norman was mumbling away in his helmet. His mother obviously didn't teach him that it was rude to speak with your mouth full. We searched him and in his boot was a black film canister full of foils of white powder. Darren and I celebrated a good punch – I mean pinch.

We took him back to our office. I told the boss that I had

him as the main suspect for causing up to three deaths that day. The boss told me that seven users had died in the previous three days.

We interviewed Norman. He was not a heroin user himself. Just making money.

He was making full admissions and all was well. At this stage I didn't want to mention the overdose deaths. I just concentrated on the trafficking.

I asked him how he packaged, cut and mixed the heroin. He was a professional and went into great detail how he purchased and how he mixed the heroin. He called it 'mixed'. He explained how he would buy the rock heroin, put it in a coffee grinder and turn the hard rock substance into a fine powder. He would then place the Glucodin into the grinder. He then told me how he would put each of the powders into foils and mix them all together.

I said, 'Hang on a second, could you tell me that again.' The interview was being taped and I needed to clarify something.

He said, 'I would buy the rock heroin and make it into a powder. Then I get the Glucodin sugar and put that in the blender too … it would then become fine like talcum powder. Then I put the heroin into foils and the sugar into foils and mix them all up.'

I said, 'You mix the 'foils' up, is that right?'

He said, 'Yes, that's how I was taught to do it properly.'

I could not believe what I was hearing.

I said, 'So you mix the foils of pure heroin with the foils of pure sugar?'

He said, 'Yep.'

I said, 'Do you ever use heroin?'

He said, 'Never. I'm not stupid.'

I walked out of the interview room. Darren shook his head and said, 'This guy killed seven drug users because he fucks up the recipe.' It was Russian Roulette, pure heroin or pure sugar.

We got a coffee and told the boss. We could not believe that his stupidity cost so many lives. I then went back into the interview room and interviewed him for several counts of manslaughter. He ended up with five years jail.

Anyway.

chapter 13

A BEAR WITH A SORE HEAD

'One golden rule of policing is that you never hit anyone else's crooks'

COPS and robbers live in a tough world. Being tough comes with the territory, but acting tough gets you into trouble. Men only ever act tough when they aren't. Some cops think that the superman suit makes them tough. They're wrong.

A good crook once told me, 'You don't get respect, you earn it.' He was right.

When I first joined the police force I had to direct traffic in the city. Whilst there I came across a bloke named Sam, although everyone knew him as Bear.

Bear looked like a shortish fat Mexican from an old western movie. He had long fuzzy hair and a long moustache. He was a key member of the Lebanese Tigers. They were a street gang that owned the footpath outside McDonalds in Swanston Street in the middle of Melbourne's central business district.

Sam was the 'gun' fighter of the Tigers. He was a bit smaller than me but he was tough. In those days Bear had to fight all the West Side Sharps, the South Side Sharps, the Tribe (Aboriginal gang) and the Carrum Boys, just to mention a few. Sam was my age but from a different world.

He had the old time crook mentality built in. He didn't have to learn it, he was born with it.

Sam lived by a code. You don't touch the very old or the very young and you treat anyone with respect who shows you respect. When I dealt with him he always knew he was a crook and that I had a job to do.

The thing I liked most about Sam was that he never had to say or do anything to 'show off' in front of his brothers like so many other street thugs. To me he deserved some respect.

Several years later I found him living around The Street. He was past his gang days. He sold a bit of gear, mostly cannabis, and handled heaps of stolen goods.

I could never catch him.

One Saturday night I was working plainclothes with Darren. Over the radio came 'Brawl outside the Wales Hotel, any units clear?'

Several police units came up on the air to attend. Darren and I just followed the speeding cop cars because they had blue lights and sirens and we didn't.

At the scene I found Bear. He was wearing his huge solid gold chain around his neck. This was no ordinary chain, each link was about the size of a ten cent piece. The whole thing weighed five ounces (140 grams). It was the biggest gold chain ever. You could have tied up the Queen Mary with it.

Bear told me that some people buy a house, but he bought a gold chain. His theory was that it was always there if he needed a large amount of money quickly. He always carried winning TAB betting slips to the value of about fifty thousand dollars that accounted for the purchase of the gold chain.

He would often say to crooks, and the odd copper, 'If you

can take it off me you can have it.' He kept it. I was standing there having a chat when Constable Tyson walked up to Bear with his note book. Tyson had taken it upon himself to take the names and addresses of everyone in the area. Tyson was a very good-looking, six foot two inch, ultra fit, immaculate, egotistical smartarse. He thought that the name Tyson meant he was tough and invincible. I don't even think he could bowl fast.

His walk alone told you everything about his personality. Tyson walked up into Bear's face and said, 'What's your name, dickhead?'

Bear looked at him and said, 'No.' He then looked at me and raised his eyebrows as if to say, 'It's not my fault, I have to do it.'

Bear then slowly lifted his right fist to get Tyson's attention then with a straight left punch hit the smartarse in the middle of his face. Tyson was out like a light before he hit the ground.

I grabbed Bear and handcuffed him. He said, 'I never showed him disrespect and he did to me.'

I said, 'I understand, Bear, but you can't just smash cops. I know he is a dickhead but you just can't.' Bear was calm and chatty. We walked off talking about the old days. Other cops walked up and saw Tyson on the ground, they all thought another cop probably did it – he was a well-known dickhead. We had to back him up, but the truth was Bear was a far better bloke than Tyson. But when you put on the uniform you have to back up everyone in blue – smartarses included.

DARREN and I were driving down Grey Street when we saw Chantel, one of our local street prostitutes. Chantel had long legs, long blonde hair with a nice bust. The whole hooker package.

Just after I drove past I looked in the rear vision mirror. A brand new BMW stopped next to her. The driver and hooker had a chat, then Chantel got into the passenger seat. I decided to have a bit of a chat to this loser.

I slowed my unmarked car down and the BMW accelerated past us, went down a couple of side streets and stopped in a deserted business car park. We pulled over. I told Darren we had time for a smoke. The plan was to let them get right into it before we bust them. I told Darren that a BMW driver was likely to pay for 'a hamburger with the lot' with extra relish.

I also allowed them extra time because it was a BMW and this meant possibly it was a European driver, likely to fiddle around a lot more. An Aussie would just get right into it, was my theory.

We got out of the car and walked up to the bouncing vehicle. They were right into it. I crept up to the driver's side door and smashed on the window. The driver nearly jumped through the roof and it wasn't a soft top. I opened the door and said, 'Relax, it's the police.'

The driver was a slimy, smooth well-dressed Greek, about twenty-five years old. He went straight onto the attack.

He said, 'What do you think you are doing?' I think it was a rhetorical question.

I said, 'I'm here because it is illegal to use a prostitute in this state.' He said, 'I hope you know this is my girlfriend. I'll have your job for this.'

I said, 'That is impossible. Not the bit about having my job, the girlfriend bit.' I looked over at Chantel and said, 'You're a bloke aren't you, Dave?'

Chantel said in a deep voice, 'Thanks, Angus.'

Up until now Chantel had spoken in high voice and sounded like one of the Bee Gees. Now she sounded like a lumberjack.

The driver nearly died. He had been having sex with Dave from behind. Dave had taken female hormones so he had breasts. He was a good looking bastard, the old Dave.

Anyway, after the initial shock, the driver fought to survive. It was as though accusing him of having sex with a prostitute was equal to murder. It was all Greek to him.

Him having just boofed a male prostitute made it hilarious for us, but not to BMW man. He wasn't sure whether to commit suicide or to kill all the witnesses.

He started to rub his head and eyes like he was trying to wash all the sexual thoughts he'd just had out of his brain.

I felt sorry for him so I said, 'Pine-o-Clean is the go, give it a good wash in Pine-o-Clean.' It was a joke, Pine-o-Clean would burn the hell out of his dick. Don't ask me how I know that.

We let Dave go and took the driver back to the station. I only ever got any fun out of the mugs in flashy cars. I used to do it because no mugs using street prostitutes meant no street prostitutes and that must be a good thing. It was our job to clean up the streets, and no-one said we couldn't have fun doing it.

VANESSA was a thirty-year-old prostitute and heroin addict. Everyone knew she was a prostitute, but you would never see her working the streets. She was a serious sort of bird with a dry sense of humour, a great body and a weatherbeaten face. It was obvious she was very intelligent by the way she spoke and the fact she could be seen reading newspapers, a very rare sight in The Street, I can tell you.

In a conversation she could snap back one liners that cut you to the quick. I often got the feeling she was streets ahead of everyone else around, including me.

She kept looking at me as though she was up to no good. I realised she wanted me to follow her. I caught up to her in a carpark around the back of the caf. She said, 'I'm getting out of this shit hole. I met this really nice truckie who lives in Alice Springs. I'm moving in with him so I leave on Friday.'

I said, 'Well, I'll see you in a month or so.'

She said, 'I don't ever want to come back. I've been thinking if I burn all my bridges here I won't be able to come back.'

I said, 'Like what?'

She said, 'Set someone up.' She was prepared to give us a good crook so she couldn't come back again.

Vanessa said, 'Pick someone good, I'll do it.'

I told her, 'I don't pay for information. I'll give you nothin'.'

She said, 'I'm doing it so I can't ever come back. What do you think?' I said, 'Well what about Cliffy?' I always wanted Cliffy.

She said, 'I don't get on with him. What about Bear?'

I said, 'You want to set Bear up?'

She said, 'Yeah, he's worth catching.' I jumped at the chance.

'You're on, ring me on my mobile at midday tomorrow. I'll come up with a plan.' She agreed and bounced off.

I stood there thinking there must be a catch, that something was wrong. I would have to watch her closely. Anyway, the following day she rang up. I worked out a cunning plan and ran with it.

Darren went with the arrest crew to the bust site. I got Vanessa to telephone Bear and tell him we wanted six pounds of cannabis at $4500 a pound. The story was that Vanessa was going to Sydney for about three months and her new boyfriend was paying for the gear.

When she sold that she would be back for more. The arrest was to happen at a service station on the outskirts of St Kilda. I drove out to pick her up. She was in Frankston.

I was running late as I had to pick up a hire car as well. I picked her up. She was her relaxed self. I was nervous, making sure everything was right. She sat there talking about how good it would be in a whole new world.

I was driving flat out, trying to get back to St Kilda to make the deal on time. As we were driving through Parkdale, Vanessa said she wanted to buy some cigarettes. I reluctantly agreed and pulled over as a small milk bar.

As she was getting out of the car she asked me for some money to buy the cigarettes. Typical. I handed her seven bucks, the required amount. She bounced away. I waited, and waited. I thought, how the hell can buying cigarettes take so long. As I burst out of the car to go and get her she burst out of the milk bar carrying two white plastic bags of goods.

I said, 'I told you no fucking stealing. Take that back.' She jumped into the passenger seat and opened the bags.

She smiled and said, 'Look I've got chips, Twisties, three packets of smokes.'

I asked, 'You robbed the milk bar man?'

She said, 'No, I boofed him.'

I said, 'We're late for a drug deal and your boofing the milk bar man.' It was ahead of its time as a way to beat the GST. The barter system was alive and well.

All the way to the drug deal she would pull some new goodie out of the bag and say, 'I've got two Bertie Beetles and look, Redskins. I love Redskins. Look, they still put the little spoon in the Whiz Fizz.' She was like a kid looking through a show bag. We got to St Kilda and I dropped her off. The plan was for her to meet up with Bear, make him sweet so he would do the deal.

I got a plainclothes cop from another station to do the deal with Bear.

We parked in the pre-arranged location and waited. Vanessa and Bear appeared out of a laneway and walked toward the car. Bear was carrying a large sports bag. He jumped into the passenger seat, Vanessa into the back.

The undercover pulled out the money, they did the deal. We drove up in cars and did the arrest. Bear turned to Vanessa, knowing it was a set up. He didn't fight, he just abused himself for falling for the whole thing.

I checked the money and the drugs. They were all there, thank Christ. Darren took Bear away and I spoke with Vanessa.

I said, 'Thanks, you did well. With his prior convictions he should get four or five years.'

She said, 'I'll send you a post card' and left.

I was wrong about Vanessa. She really did just want to get away from the street. With Bear the way he was, there was no way she could ever come back. I went back to the station. It was a good pinch.

Bear was very, very unhappy about the whole thing.

He said no comment to everything in the interview. At one

stage Darren went and made a coffee. We came back a few minutes later.

Bear was bleeding from the nose and obviously had been bashed. I asked him what happened, and he said, 'Nothin.'

One golden rule of policing is that you never ever hit anyone else's crook. You're allowed to hit your own but never someone else's. I had seen Tyson in the hallway. He still had a black eye with a cut above it. I knew Bear wouldn't complain. He wasn't the type.

We forgot about it and moved on. Later, he was remanded in custody. I had to take him to his cell and Bear was not his jovial self. He was seething mad over what Vanessa had done to him.

As I was closing the door to his cell he spoke, 'You should be charged with being an accessory and conspiracy.'

I said, 'How do you work that out?'

Bear said, 'Don't you know?'

I said, 'Know what?'

He said, 'Just before we walked up to the car and got busted Vanessa asked me if she could wear my gold chain for a second, and I let her.' I said, 'You're kidding?'

We both laughed. I pulled out a smoke and gave him one.

Bear smiled and said, 'She got me twice, that smartarse bitch.'

I said, 'What a pisser, so that's what it was all about.' We laughed. Bear knew I knew nothing about her plan.

Vanessa had about $30,000 worth of pure gold. The truckie in Alice Springs had scored a treasure trove. Presuming, of course, that's where she went.

The moral of the story is never trust a street crow who reads newspapers.

DARREN and I were on the move in an unmarked police car, when we noticed a vehicle driving without its lights on. I did a U-turn, Darren put the blue light on the roof, the car pulled over and we drew up alongside.

The driver was a young, beautiful Japanese girl. Darren wound his window down and said, 'It's dark, isn't it.'

She said, 'Yes it is.'

I drove off. She sat there for a moment. In my rear vision mirror I saw her headlights go on.

She then chased us and pulled us over. She said that she had been having trouble with a peeping tom. We followed her to her flat, which was on the first floor. She brought us inside, and showed us her bathroom. She pointed out her window, which overlooked a small laneway.

She said that when she had a shower in the morning a man would stop and watch her from the lane. She told us that she had her shower at 7.30am each day. We said we'd be there.

The following morning we arrived in the lane early. We stood there and watched her take her tiny little nightie off and get into the shower. She was stunning. Drop dead gorgeous. We stood there mesmerised. We could see her beautiful shape through the glass shower recess. Moments later, the offender walked up the lane. He was wearing a suit and carrying a brief case. He stopped next to us. The three of us stood there looking up at her. The offender said, 'I'm late. It wasn't the little light blue nightie was it?'

I said, 'It was the little light blue nightie.'

Moments later she got out, dried herself and left the bathroom.

The offender said, 'See you tomorrow morning.'

I said, 'Sure mate, see ya.'

We went upstairs. She was all wet, wrapped in a towel.

I said, 'We fixed the problem. He won't be coming back.' I lied.

The following day we drove down the lane in the middle of the day, just in case. I noticed she had put a blind on the window, blocking any future views. Bummer.

Later that week I found out why. Darren brought her to dinner at my place.

THE following day Bear went to court and got bail. His associates put up a large surety. I was at my office doing paperwork, but Darren was busting to go out and catch crooks. Eventually, we went to the police station to sign out a couple of firearms. It was 3pm, right on the change of shift.

Tyson had finished work. He walked past me mumbling something under his breath. We signed out our guns and went back out to our car. As we got to our car I heard a muffled sound.

I walked over between some cars and found Tyson lying on the ground, bleeding. He said through a mouthful of fat lips, 'It was Bear.' Tyson was only bashed. He was going to be all right. The good part was he now had two black eyes and a badly bruised face.

He staggered back into the station while we went looking for Bear. Tyson was a dickhead, but you can't bash cops. We searched everywhere but found nothing.

We went to his wife's house, girlfriend's house, all his common hangouts, but came up empty. We found that Bear was bailed out from court at 11am. One of his conditions of bail was that he must report to St Kilda Police Station between 9am to 9pm every day. He had reported to the station on bail just before he bashed Tyson. We couldn't find the Bear anywhere, so we went home.

The following day Darren and I were at our office. It was about 10am and I was telling everyone the story about dickhead Tyson, how he had punched a handcuffed Bear and how the crook had met him on an even playing field and bashed him back.

Meanwhile, back at St Kilda Police Station, the front door opened, and into the watchhouse area walked Bear. He casually walked up to the counter and said, 'Can I have the bail book I have to sign.'

The watchhouse keeper stepped backwards, ignoring his request. In shock he bent down and pushed the intercom button and said in a loud voice, 'Attention all members, attention all members, all members to the watch-house NOW.'

Cool to the end, Bear lifted his pen in his right hand as if to say I still need to sign on. The watchhouse keeper gave him the book, Bear signed on as all the cops in the station arrived. Bear didn't fight. He just got bashed.

At the end of it all someone pulled Tyson off him. Bear lay on the floor, bleeding and cuffed while about fifteen uniform members stood around, looking at him.

Bear became a legend that day. He earned the respect of every cop in the district. Crooks also heard what happened. Bear never had to fight again. Everyone also knew about Tyson – that he was a pretend tough guy who could only beat up a guy when he was handcuffed and backed up by fifteen coppers.

THERE once was a crook named Boyd. He was thirty years old, tall and ugly. He was a heroin-addicted burglar who had one big advantage. His dad was a locksmith, so he grew up learning how to walk through locked doors.

Anyway, I got some red hot mail that Boyd had stolen a safe in a factory burglary in Northcote. Boyd lived in a big, two-storey house in East St Kilda with three other crooks. We all knew Boyd and his house well because, for different reasons, we had raided it three times in the previous month.

I decided to raid the house as soon as possible rather than wait for the usual 4am start. I held an impromptu briefing. Minutes later, four cars double parked outside the house and we climbed out in a busy side street. We were all fully kitted up with vests, sledge hammer, and a couple of shotguns – the lot. Like the Boy Scouts, we wanted to be prepared.

As we walked onto the footpath, we got into our allotted positions. Paul with one strike of the door made it fall flat into the hallway. It had no hinges. He then stepped back.

Darren stepped into the hall, placed a large portable Disco Robo sound system against the left side wall and pushed the play button.

The landing music from the movie *Apocalypse Now* blasted through the house as we entered. It was sensational. As true professionals, we walked at a controlled steady pace clearing one room at a time. Well, that was the plan. The reality was, we all just ran in all directions screaming and smashing into each other until we got tired. For some reason it's more fun that way.

There was no-one home. The loud music would have had a great effect on anyone that was home but, sadly, they were out on burglar business. On the inside of the back door was a post card with a picture of a pig's face on it.

Under the card was the name of our officer in charge of our

CIB office. I walked out the back. About five metres from the back door was a small shed. On the door of the shed there was a big 'Keep Out' sign, so I kicked it. It didn't budge. Paul saw me and said, 'I'll get the key.'

He turned toward the back door, where there was an axe leaning against the wall of the house. He picked it up and hit the middle of the door as hard as he could.

The axe cut the door neatly in half. We pulled it open and walked in. As we started to search the shed I noticed blue and white string hanging either side of the door.

One end of the string was tied to a nail. The other was tied to a small piece of wood that was in the jaws of a clothes peg. The clothes peg had wires attached to it, the wires were attached to a battery, the battery had a wire that went into a small souvenir style liquor bottle labelled Irish Whisky. The bottle was full of white powder.

What I was looking at was a bomb.

I realised that the axe had gone through the door and cut the string, if I had managed to kick it open or hit it with a sledge hammer it would have detonated. Paul was still looking around.

I said, 'Paul, don't move, there's a bomb here.' Paul and I tiptoed out of the shed and warned everyone.

Darren said, 'Where is it, can I have a look?'

I said, 'You want to have a look at a bomb?' Paul wanted to put it in a bucket of water or something because he had seen that in a movie. I had a better idea. I wanted to get right away from it.

We called the SOG. They came down and made it safe, then it was taken out to forensic and detonated. The boffin said it would have killed everyone in the vicinity of the shed and in the back of the house.

The expert also said, 'This bomb has been taken directly from a book called *James Bond's book of Medicine* – an American book written by anarchists.

We searched the house again, this time looking for evidence. There was nothing there. The only other address we could connect to Boyd was his mother's home in Malvern.

We took out a warrant and began leaving the station to execute it on his mum's house. As we were leaving I looked at my partner and said, 'Ah, Darren, I um, don't really think we need that.' He dropped his head and reluctantly turned around and carried the Disco Robo sound system back into our office.

We got to the house, knocked on the door and a lovely old women opened it. She invited us in. We explained we were looking for her son. She understood he had a drug problem. On the television I noticed a collection of small liquor bottles from all over Britain. There was a dustless circle indicating one bottle was missing. We then located the book we were looking for, and the wire etc. The only thing we didn't have was Boyd.

I found several small black canisters with a plastic grip attached to them. They were strange little spray packs.

I said to Paul, 'I'll just test it.'

Paul said, 'You're not going to smell it, are you?'

I said, 'No, don't be stupid.'

I did a little spray toward the doorway and stepped back. I then called out, 'Darren, come in here for a second.' The trusting soul walked into the room. I asked him, 'Can you smell?' Just as I said that Darren grabbed his throat and fell to the ground. I said, 'I thought it was mace … I was just trying to work out what it was.' Darren didn't look happy, but he couldn't complain. He was too busy choking.

We photographed and video-taped everything. Back in St

Kilda Darren and I went looking for the informer that told us about Boyd doing the safe job.

It turned out that Boyd himself had been spouting off to everyone that he'd done a safe job. We could never find out which job it was. That's because there never was a safe job. Boyd just wanted us to raid his house again so he could blow us up. The search for him intensified.

He was nowhere to be seen.

About two weeks later we stopped to get lunch at a take-away shop in The Street. I went to the toilet, Darren was standing in line to be served. The man in front of him had purchased his food, picked it up and turned around. Darren looked at him face to face. It was Boyd.

They instantly recognised each other. Boyd let go of his food and reached for his gun, which was tucked into the front of his pants. Darren reached for his gun in its shoulder holster, but it wasn't there because he didn't have one.

Boyd levelled the gun at his face and pulled the trigger. It went 'click'. Nothing happened.

Boyd stepped forward, slamming his gun into Darren's face with such force it pushed him back two steps into the large glass front window.

It was safety glass and it exploded into a thousand pieces. Boyd followed Darren through the window, falling on top of him. Darren helped break Boyd's fall. While my partner rolled around in the glass trying to get up, Boyd left the scene. Fast.

I came out of the toilet and saw the mayhem. Darren was concussed. I lifted him up out of the glass. By now people were everywhere. He said, 'Boyd tried to kill me. I could have sworn I signed out a gun this morning.'

I said, 'You did.' I lifted the bottom of his jacket and there was his gun in a holster on his belt. I said, 'Remember you forgot your shoulder holster and put on a belt one instead?'

Lesson: When you get used to one thing, stick to it. When an emergency happens and you have to react instinctively you instantly do what you have done time and time again. The moment Darren found his gun was not where his reflexes told him it should be, he decided he had no gun. The simple mistake of forgetting his shoulder holster almost cost him his life.

Everyone searched for Boyd, but we didn't get a sniff. I decided to look for an old girlfriend of his, only because there was nowhere else to look. Darren and I sat off her house. We watched her leave and followed her. She ended up at a restaurant. We sat back. It was hopeless, nothing. All of a sudden a car double parked and a dark figure walked in. I said to Darren that I was going to have a closer look.

The driver's hair was all wrong. It was black and too short. I saw him talking to the old girlfriend. He turned and looked straight at me. It was Boyd. He turned toward the rear door of the restaurant. Darren was standing there. I was just inside the front door. I started to draw my revolver, and he drew his gun from his pants then ran straight at the front window.

As he got to the window he dived head first into it. He hit the window in full flight, head first, CRASH. It held firm, like a brick wall. It barely even flexed when he hit it. Boyd bounced off it like a wet sock, fell to the floor in a crumpled heap and didn't move. It might work in the movies, but not in St Kilda.

The Italian manager of the restaurant screamed, 'What he do, this idiot.' The food wasn't that bad.

Boyd's girlfriend screamed, 'You've killed him, you bastards.'

Covering him with my handgun, I walked up and stood on his wrist, bent down and took his pistol from his hand. I made it safe and tucked it into my pants. I cuffed his lifeless body – nothing like being safe. People in the restaurant were still screaming when I lifted my portable radio and called for an ambulance. Darren walked up, looked me in the eyes and smiled. He was a happy camper.

The manager was a middle-aged, hard-working Italian. He walked up to Boyd's lifeless body and started to abuse him.

He said, 'These idiots my window she break one time, two time so I spend more money and get good quality. This one window even hammer she no break'. She broke Boyd instead.

We charged him with everything: Set explosives, attempted murder of Darren and every other charge we could think of. A month later he died in prison of a heroin overdose while awaiting trial. No great loss.

chapter 14

A CUNNING STUNT

**'You have to know The Street and become part of it
... there was always criminal activity there'**

MARIELLE was very attractive. Her good looks distracted cops and crooks alike. She kept very fit and had a body to die for. Marielle was a constable about twelve months junior to me.

We had a gym in the station that nobody used. Our bicep curls were done in the pub, lifting pots of beer.

That was until Marielle decided to start working out. From then on the gym was packed. I recall straining to pick up the hand piece of the telephone after lifting grossly excessive weights trying to impress her.

While working plainclothes I became aware of a flasher exposing himself in Alma Park. His modus operandi was to walk up to female sun bathers and masturbate near them. At times right above them. He was a real toff.

I knew the park well. It was beautiful, with a large well-kept grass area in the middle surrounded by huge trees.

It was open enough for women to feel safe, yet enclosed enough to be private. On any sunny day women could be seen soaking up the sun. I thought of a cunning plan. My plan needed bait and Marielle would be perfect. I asked the sergeant if I could use her for a while, and he agreed. My plan was perfect except that about ten minutes after I hatched it the sun disappeared. It took forever before the sun came out again.

Well, three hours, anyway. By this time Marielle had been able to drive home to collect what she called her 'gear'.

Her gear was in a large sports bag. Darren and I grabbed our stuff and we all left. Several members asked us what we were doing. I mumbled something about us going to a private function. Darren and I decided to keep this one to ourselves. There were times for back-up and this was not one of them.

At the park the three of us walked into a small gable-roofed pergola situated on the south edge of the grass area.

I said, 'We'll have the briefing in here. This will be the command post. Now Darren and I will sit in here pretending to be a couple of pissheads drinking cans and talking shit while you walk out in the middle there and work on your tan.'

Marielle thought it was a great idea. She said, 'Now, he is about thirty-five, Australian, long brown hair with a large pot belly, right?'

I said, 'He'll be the one with his dick out.' I then screwed up my face pushing my lips as close as I could to my nose and said, 'His face will look like this.'

Darren and I both laughed. I qualified that by saying, 'Well, that's what I've been told a bloke looks like when he's masturbating. I wouldn't know.' I was trying to impress her with my wit. It wasn't working.

Marielle said, 'Yeah, right.' She looked bored. She

opened up my esky, took out a cold can of bourbon and coke and walked out into the middle of the park and looked for a nice patch of grass.

As she walked off I called out to her, 'Monitor channel two.' I was trying to impress her with my professionalism. It wasn't working.

I sat back on the bench, cracked open a can and said, 'Right, let's start pretending.' Handing Darren a can, I said: 'My plan is to drink a few of these cans, then fill them up with coke or something and sit here pretending to drink real cans like real yobbos so we don't look like cops. What do you think?'

Darren tuned into the cricket on his little transistor radio, sat back and said, 'Perfect.'

Now this was what I joined the job for. No freezing nights hiding in frontyards trying to catch druggies. Sitting there drinking bourbon and coke in the sun while perving on a near-nude girl was clearly the go. And we got paid for it.

We watched as Marielle stopped, opened her bag and removed a large beach towel. She carefully laid it out on the grass. She dropped her dress to the ground revealing tiny little bikini pants. She then stood there and removed her bra while she still had her T-shirt on.

Darren mumbled, 'That's incredible, how do they do that?'

I said, 'I still have trouble putting my shoulder holster on.' Darren felt his shoulder holster under his shirt, sat forward and tried to work out how to do it.

Back to Marielle. She said down on the towel and started removing about ten bottles and containers. I grabbed our small telescope and zoomed up on them. I said, 'They're sun tan lotions.' Darren said, 'What?' and promptly grabbed the scope from me.

I said, 'I had no idea sun baking was so bloody technical.' She then began to slowly rub the different sun protection stuff onto different parts of her body. Darren and I were entranced. It was as though he had just discovered the meaning of life. He said, 'Oh, I geddit. Those bits must need a higher protection factor.'

I said, 'If she keeps that up we'll get more than just our target.'

Darren said, 'If he doesn't hurry, I'll be out there.'

I said, 'If I have to arrest you, can I borrow your cuffs, mine are back at the office?'

Marielle reached into her bag again and produced an old-fashioned alarm clock. It was the type with the two little bells on top. I said, 'She is a professional, mate.'

I knew it wouldn't take long. Two large blokes struggling with an esky staggered toward us. I looked at them and said, 'Shit, did you tell the CI?' Darren said, 'No way.'

Our CIB had somehow heard of our operation. These two looked like the reconnaissance team. Minutes later several other detectives arrived. They set up camp a few metres behind us. When we needed them for surveillance at night they were nowhere to be found. But when it came to a pretty, half-naked girl they were there in droves. It was obvious that their main aim was not to protect the public as much as it was to observe our bait.

About ten minutes later her little alarm rang out. She reset it and turned over onto her side moving around on her towel to expose a whole new section of her body to the sun.

A small cheer rang out from the gallery each time she moved. Darren said, 'And to think I thought sun baking was just lying out in the sun.'

Over the next hour numerous boys and men took huge detours to walk past Marielle to have a perve. After an hour we got sick of saying, 'Here he is, I think this is him.' None of them was the offender. Darren crushed his empty can and threw it out onto the lawn in front of us. I said, 'What?'

Darren said, 'I'm a yobbo.' Darren was having a ball. I looked up and noticed a small thin dark-skinned bloke stop and appear to talk to Marielle.

I noticed she had undone the strap of her bikini top. She was lying face down wearing nothing but her tiny bikini bottoms. This unknown male then walked off on his way.

I picked up the radio and said, 'Angus to Muzza, what's his go.' Marielle said, 'His line was, "Would you like to share the sun with me?" I said to him, "I think not" and he walked off.'

I said, 'If you want a break sing out.'

Marielle said, 'I'm okay. I finish work in about half an hour. I suppose I could do some overtime.'

I noticed a bloke was heading straight back toward Marielle. He walked up behind her and was out of her sight. She was reading a book facing away from him.

He undid his pants in a flash and produced a large erection. He looked quite proud of it, actually. He began to sway from side to side pulling on his penis as fast as he could.

I jumped to my feet and began to sprint at him. I first tried not to spill my can, then I realised I didn't need it and threw it aside. I was doing well until I caught the guy's eye.

He looked at me running straight at him. He burst into a

sprint after putting the trouser snake away. As he did I screamed, 'Muzza.' She looked up and saw him begin to run. Marielle jumped up and gave chase.

I recall the sight in slow motion. I remember as if it was yesterday.

As a matter of fact I did remember it yesterday.

Marielle had undone the back strap of her bikini top. This gave her breasts no support, so they bounced heavily. She then put her right arm across her right breast and took a firm grip of the left one.

I knew if I was ever to be allowed to do this sort of operation in the future we had to catch the crook, not the lure. It didn't really matter that he wasn't 'our' crook. An arrest would be a bonus.

Cops are like seagulls and sheep. One moves, we all move. I heard the spectating detectives begin to give chase. But they were definitely chasing the bait.

They ran because the bait ran. Our friend the mystery masturbator looked over his shoulder and saw everyone in the whole park chasing him.

He ran straight at Alma Road. By now it was about 5pm, peak hour.

Darren passed me running flat out. The bourbon and cokes were slowing me down. Our tosser ran straight out into traffic. Two cars just missed him.

Marielle stopped just short of the gutter. In doing so, to save her balance, she let go of her breasts. Drivers paused to look, then the cars behind them slammed on their brakes to avoid collision.

As brakes screeched our suspect looked back at Marielle. The sight of her made him stop. Darren, running at full sprint, poleaxed him to the ground. The arrest was completed. He was stiff to be caught.

I eventually crossed the road and took possession of our catch. He wasn't much, but I suppose he was something. He was that small I should have thrown him back. He appeared to be harmless until he opened his mouth.

I said, 'Listen, sunshine, you're not obliged to say anything but anything …'

He interrupted: 'Let me go. I am a solicitor.' Funny, to me he looked African. I said, 'I don't give a toss, even if you do. You are busted, now shut up while I'm trying to tell you your rights.'

Sunshine said, 'I have done nothing. I am an Egyptian citizen. I am a solicitor, let me go.'

I asked him what his mummy would think of what he had done. He didn't get it. We charged him with wilful and obscene behavior. He was not a happy man.

Knowing that his career was on the line he fought the charges with everything he had. He was found guilty, suspended from acting as a solicitor and fined $500. It was a good result.

He appealed. At the County Court a jury found him not guilty. He was reinstated as a solicitor and is still practising today.

St Kilda days were great. Incidents like the one with Marielle and our day in the sun made them special. Marielle went on to marry a colourful detective inspector known as The Rocket. He is a very lucky man. They have two lovely kids. Good luck to them.

MY girlfriend and I decided to have a dinner party with friends. I invited Mark, a bank manager, and Vince, the bricklayer, and their wives. The six of us used to take it in turns to have dinner at each other's houses and it was our turn.

We started talking about the usual stuff people talk to cops about: drugs, crime and how best to stop both. Mark and his wife Nicky lived in St Kilda. They said they never see prostitutes, drug addicts or criminals. None of it.

They said they see some 'bad' types, but not criminals. Mark could not understand what I was on about. I kept telling them that St Kilda was out of control, crime wise.

Vince apparently hadn't seen real crooks anywhere, either, let alone St Kilda, except on TV being led into court. He did say he was offered some stolen stereo equipment at work once.

Vince said he'd punched the bloke in the head and dragged him off the building site.

Vince worked hard for his money and paid tax, so he hated crooks as much as he hated dole bludgers.

Anyway, this night my girlfriend had meticulously prepared a taste sensation – crab quiche. As the guests arrived they commented on the incredible aroma of the fresh crab.

These were big sand crabs or swimmer crabs. I explained how I had risked life and limb catching each crab by hand underwater, scuba diving. How I saw the eyes sticking out of the sand, estimated where the claws would be, then grabbed each claw.

I explained how I'd brought them home, boiled them up, sat in front of the cricket and removed all the crab meat by hand and put it in a bowl ready for my girlfriend 'Harry' (Harriet). When entree was ready we solved a few more of the world's problems, then made our way to the dinner table.

Harry brought the entree. It was fresh crab mixed with chopped fresh scallops and small pieces of rockling, carefully put in a soup.

I had dived out off Sandringham and collected a heap of scallops then dived off Black Rock and got a large spotted rockling.

I had gone to the Bentleigh Market and bought five large chicken carcasses, simmered them with onions and herbs for four hours and made the stock, reducing it to a couple of litres, then added the fresh crab, scallops and rockling.

When it was almost cooked I added finely sliced egg omelette after slowly dribbling two egg whites through the soup – and, finally, sliced shallots, a bay leaf and assorted spices. The result was to die for. Several fish and crustaceans already had.

While we ate the entree we were consumed by the moment. The atmosphere was warm and close. This is what life is all about, friends talking about everyday family things … such as one of their young daughters being taken to the toilet by her mum wearing 'in-line' skates and the young girl telling her, 'Be careful mum – don't get poo on my wheels.'

I found myself bragging about why the food was so good, why it was all so fresh and why their tastebuds were overdosing.

I said, 'A lot of people individually select their seafood through the chilled glass window of the local fish shop. My window is my mask.'

Sure, I was showing off, but I got enjoyment from the hunter-gatherer bit. No harm in that, I suppose.

These moments are what life is all about. They gave me perspective.

We were a world away from The Street – and it was a relief. I wallowed in the normality, hoping to wash away the evil that had become part of my daily life. It was a wake-up call to remind me not everyone was a criminal or a crime victim.

Our tastebuds were still recovering when Harry opened the oven. The fresh crab quiche was a perfect light golden brown. The aroma was mouth-watering.

Harry was wearing a small oven glove. She put her hand under the metal tray, gently lifted it off the metal shelf and began to turn toward the kitchen bench. The hot outer metal ring of the quiche dish came away from the pastry and base and fell down onto her inner forearm.

As the soft skin burnt she threw the quiche into the air and squealed with pain. The quiche landed with a splash on the bench and then the floor – face down, of course. Overwhelmed with embarrassment and pain, Harry fell to her knees, crying. Nicky and Sally immediately consoled her.

I mumbled something about two large pizzas and we left. We went in Vincent's beaten-up old Ford Fairlane. I ordered the pizzas on my mobile phone. Vince drove, Mark sat in the front passenger seat and I sat in the back. I told them I would take them on a tour of their precious St Kilda.

We drove down Grey, Acland and Barkly Streets. I pointed out prostitutes, petty crooks and drug dealers, not to mention a few well-known local idiots. I gave them a running commentary while watching two cops who had no idea what they were doing.

The two cops could not see what was going on around

them – they were like tourists. Deals were going down in front of them and they couldn't see. I said that to be a cop you have to know The Street and become part of it.

I explained how much fun it was to catch crooks and said there was always criminal activity there. You just had to know where to look.

I directed Vincent to double-park right out the front of the St Kilda Cafe. I held my left hand over my face and told the other two to look inside and when they got eye contact, to nod.

All of a sudden Mark the bank manager screamed, 'Quick go, go! Get out of here. Here comes one! Go, go.' Vincent started to drive off but I told him to stop and learn. A large and very aggressive female walked straight up to the window, looked Mark in the face and said, 'What do ya want – smack?'

I had never seen her before. Her face was about three inches from Mark's. He froze with fear. She then held a foil of heroin up to his face and said, 'Give me $90 and go.'

Mark couldn't breathe. She then said, 'Okay, ya can have two for $160 and that's it.'

Mark said, 'Go.' Vincent accelerated off. As we left, the female trafficker yelled abuse at us.

I sat up in the seat and said, 'There you go, crooks up close and personal.' Mark was in shock. Vincent raved on about how he couldn't believe how she offered us heroin like that.

We stopped down the street a bit to buy smokes. They voted I leave the safety of the vehicle to buy them. I laughed. When we got home they had great stories to tell their wives.

I was happy. I had given them a little peek at my world. But it had also given me a flash of insight into myself ... I realised The Street had hold of me and that if I stayed out there too long I'd rather be with the freaks than with decent people.

Name ...... M:CULLOCH L.N.. Reg. No. ...2+205..................

REMARKS BY OFFICER IN CHARGE OF DISTRICT AS TO CONDUCT AND EFFICIENCY, RECOMMENDATIONS, ETC.

(To be entered on transfer, discharge, dismissal or death of member or when Officer in Charge of District transfers, or retires. See Regulations 278 and 279.)

Date	Comment
30.1.86	Appointment confirmed.
22.4.86	A keen, well conducted member with a good work performance. A BOLTON, Chief Superintendent.
17/11/1986	"Commended at District level for observation, initiative and diligence displayed in the detection and apprehension of two offenders for a number of offences, and in the recovery of a substantial amount of stolen property."
23/3/87	"Commended at District Level for initiative, diligence and attention to duty in following up a casual remark which they overheard and which resulted in the detection and arrest of two offenders for a car theft which would otherwise have gone undetected." J. FRAME (Assistant commissioner) File No. 13-3-3841
1987 25/10/88	Passed Theoretical (Law) Examination. P/G 12/11/87 A well conducted, effective member who performed his duty at St.Kilda in a highly satisfactory manner. R. F. GILL Chief Superintendent

VICTORIA POLICE

RESIGNATION BY DETECTIVE SENIOR CONSTABLE LACHLAN NEIL MC CULLOCH 24205 FROM THE VICTIORIA POLICE FORCE.

1.   I joined the Victoria Police Force on the 31st January the 31st, 1984. I have had an absolute ball over the past 16 years. I am proud to have been a member of the Victoria Police Force.

2.   It's now time for me to move on to my next career. I therefore forward my resignation effective as of 20 November, 1999.

L.McCULLOCH
Detective Senior Constable 24205

SEXUAL CRIMES SQUAD
CORRO No 404/99
DATE 22 / 11 /99